Praise for

Finding Freedom... Finding Me

Finding Freedom... Finding Me *is an engrossing true story of one woman's journey through more traumas than many of us will ever have. I couldn't put this inspirational book down, captivated by the author's refreshingly raw honesty through her painful journey of emotional healing as she evolved into self-love and self-acceptance. She also engages the reader more with 'For You to Ponder' questions at the end of each chapter. A great read!*

Michelle Mayur
Spiritual teacher, healer and author of Embraced by the Divine: The Emerging Woman's Gateway to Power, Passion and Purpose
www.embracedbythedivine.com

Jody's book is beautifully written and is a genuine outpouring of the heart. She writes of her past as it really was, with an honesty and frankness which is sometimes confronting but always engaging. It is a true story of triumph over difficult events and numerous setbacks, in which a steadfast resilience shows through. Each chapter has helpful questions for consideration, encouraging the reader to reflect on their own life journey. This book is a powerful catalyst for inner transformation.

Grant Lambert
Advanced Alchemy Pty Ltd
www.qualityessences.com

An incredible journey both inward and outward! Courageously speaking her truth, Jody Kalpenos writes a compelling and honest story about her journey from pain to joy. By doing so, she helps others look deep within themselves to uncover and heal their own stuffed emotions, internal woundings and darkest fears. Using a simple journaling technique, along with asking good questions, Jody helps the reader to explore and unravel their inner world, enabling them to clarify and heal their life from the inside out with compassion and love.

Cindy Powers Prosor
The Intuitive Heart Mentor
www.openingdoorswithin.com

Jody's memoir is a brave account of her journey through healing trauma, crisis and transformation. She generously takes the reader into her inner world, and has been incredibly vulnerable in sharing a story that turned her inside out. She shares moments of inspiration and courage from her journey so that the reader may find support and insight to apply in their own moments of challenge. Jody encourages readers to delve deeply and to take the path of transformation, and to help with this she provides self-enquiry journaling questions to encourage those who are ready to take the next step.

Martina Hughes
Tantric Blossoming
www.tantricblossoming.com

If you've ever felt as though you don't belong or don't fit in, or you've been seeking love in all the 'wrong' places, let Jody take you on a deeply transformational journey in which she shares her challenges and triumphs in a beautiful story of travelling to find herself. Despite some pretty intense challenges, she ultimately thrives. Through reading her raw and vulnerable truth, may you also experience the profound freedom of coming home to yourself, of opening yourself up to express your authentic truth in the world.

Tina van Leuven
The Joy Oracle
www.innerdelight.com

෴

Jody Kalpenos writes a raw and very real revelation of her life, sharing her journey through deep loss and inner struggle to accomplishment. Her book is not just a memoir; it is also a workbook to help people come to terms with deep issues, and to assist in the healing process. The greatest teachers are those who have overcome the greatest challenges. This is a must-read.

Brenda Pearce
Author & CEO of eFactor Media;
Partner in Wisdoms From the Heart Publications
www.efactorlive.com; www.wisdomsfromtheheart.com

෴

When we are children we are poorly equipped to handle the circumstances that we are dealt. As adults we get to choose between living as a victim or learning to stand in our power. Jody travels us through her very personal experiences as she chooses to exit from unintentionally living as a victim to, instead, standing tall as she blossoms into personal power. Powerful artwork sprinkled through her story beautifully expresses Jody's deep inner feelings. Similar to badly treated soil, deep wounds can be healed, with miraculous results. This is a beautifully raw book that drew me deeper, and offered questions to ponder.

Linda Murray
Cosmic Connector
www.carbiculture.com/dancing-with-nature

Finding Freedom… Finding Me takes the reader deep into the heart of Jody's personal story and shows us how, through her pain, heartache and loss, she has found freedom and inner peace.

I love and respect the rawness and openness of Jody's writing. You feel like you are journeying with her. There were many times when I felt deeply moved by her courage and resilience. There is so much in this book that that I could relate to – relationships, family, parenting, love, life's purpose.

You will love this book if you are looking for a female role model to inspire you. Jody has not only provided readers with an intimate glimpse into her own life challenges, but at the end of most chapters she has provided a guide for us to contemplate and work through our own.

Victoria Wilding
Coach, mentor, speaker & author
www.victoriawilding.com, www.shiftfoundation.org

Finding Freedom...
Finding Me

An Extraordinary Journey Out of Pain and Darkness Into Love and Light

Jody Kalpenos

First published in 2015 by Jody Kalpenos
PO Box 621, Yarraville Vic 3013

© Jody Kalpenos 2015

The moral rights of the author have been asserted.

National Library of Australia Cataloguing-in-Publication entry:
Creator: Kalpenos, Jody, author.
Title: *Finding Freedom... Finding Me* : an extraordinary journey out of pain and darkness into love and light / Jody Kalpenos.
ISBN: 9780994370709 (paperback)
9780994370716 (ebook: Kindle)
9780994370730 (ebook: epub)
Subjects: Kalpenos, Jody.
Self-actualization (Psychology).
Self-realization.
Life skills.
Spiritual biography.
Dewey Number: 158.1

All rights reserved. Except as permitted under international copyright laws, no part of this book may be reproduced in any form or by any means, be stored in a retrieval system, or be communicated or transmitted in any form or by any means, without prior written permission. All enquiries should be made to the publisher at the above address.

Publishing consultancy and editing: Rich Life by Design
Cover illustration and design: Amy De Wolfe
Cover photography: Edyta Pawlowska, Pelevina Ksinia
Interior design and layout: Amy De Wolfe
Author photo: Jade Wisely Photography

Disclaimer
The author of this book does not dispense medical advice or prescribe the use of any technique as a form of treatment for physical, emotional or medical problems without the advice of a physician, either directly or indirectly. The intent of the author is only to offer information of a general nature to help you in your quest for emotional and spiritual wellbeing. In the event that you use the information in this book for yourself, the author assumes no responsibility for your actions. The author's opinions throughout the book are hers alone, and no third party has endorsed her comments.

Dedicated to

James and Liam ~ my ultimate teachers, my greatest blessing

*'You alone are enough.
You have nothing to prove to anybody.'*

~ Maya Angelou

Table of Contents

Foreword		13
Introduction		17
Chapter 1:	A Dam Tragedy	23
Chapter 2:	Running Free	31
Chapter 3:	The Flame of Terror	39
Chapter 4 :	A Deep Chasm Opens Up	49
Chapter 5:	The Wider World Calls to Me	57
Chapter 6:	Big Ben, Baguettes & Bananas	67
Chapter 7:	Motherhood Challenges Me	83
Chapter 8:	Help Me, Please!	91
Chapter 9:	I Did It Before Gwyneth	101
Chapter 10:	Betrayal Breaks Me	109
Chapter 11:	Family Catastrophe	117
Chapter 12:	Circle of Gratitude	125
Chapter 13:	A Letter to My Boys	131
Chapter 14:	My Best Friend, Resilience	135
Chapter 15:	I Heed the Call of a Gallic Song	147
Chapter 16:	Learning to Love & Accept Myself	157
Chapter 17:	A Heart Cracked Open	169
Chapter 18:	Creating a New Melody	181
Chapter 19:	Taking Flight	187
Chapter 20:	What Is the Meaning of It All?	197
The Power of Journaling: A Guide to Getting Started		201
For You to Delve Deeper...		205

Circle of Gratitude: Creating Your Own Ceremony	213
My Heartfelt Thanks	217
My Healing Team	223
Feed Your Mind & Soul	225
About the Author	229

Foreword

I remember the first time Jody ventured into my yoga class in 2008. Her pain was evident behind the mask of 'I'm fine'; she was hanging on tight just in case she broke down. With regular yoga and energy healing, the cracks slowly began to appear, the mask was removed and she didn't break down... she broke through!

Today, she is a new woman, alive with passion and purpose, living her truth, standing in her power and sharing her wisdom in her life's work.

In this, her beautiful book, you will be drawn into a powerful story – from a childhood of grief, loss and survival to a life of beauty, healing, motherhood, discovery and truth.

The wounds of the trauma are often invisible to the naked eye but are felt deeply by the survivor. These wounds are very rarely understood until a woman is ready to move from being a survivor to a thriver. *Finding Freedom... Finding Me* honours the little girl who lived through trauma, and in doing so, gives hope to women around the world.

My own story, with its thoughts, memories and a few niggly bits, began to surface while I read this book. At first I tried to quieten them so I could stay true to Jody's story but then I realised this is the gold within the book. Jody's sharing of her story and her gentle encouragement for you to reflect on your own life work in tandem to help you to heal, too.

Finding Freedom… Finding Me goes beyond being an autobiography – it becomes something so much more personal, like a conversation with a close friend who shares her story in a safe space and then invites you to share yours… *uninterrupted*.

The book speaks directly to the wounded hearts of survivors of childhood trauma who became the grade A student, the rescuer, the peacekeeper, smiling when she wanted to cry, putting herself last, the 'yes' girl, never getting angry and definitely never rocking the boat.

That girl grew up and became the woman who felt empty and tried to fill the vacuum with things, food, drink and bad relationships. Everyone used to shake their head… what is wrong with that woman? What is missing from her life? Who is she searching for? The answer is… *herself!*

Jody shares honestly how deep family loss affected her. She could have kept Pandora's box tightly shut but she chose to heal, to stand up when it would have been easier to sit down and shut up. Why? Because she knew her story could help other women.

As the book draws to a close there is a definite shift in tone as Jody re-discovers her *joie de vivre*. You can feel the words leap off the page as she shares her passion for France, her joy for motherhood, the opening of her heart to love and the creation of a business that embodies her knowledge, passion, inspiration and wisdom.

Finding Freedom… Finding Me is a journey of healing, discovery, love, motherhood and everything in between. It will bring you into the present moment, which is rich with possibility, inspiration and wonder.

Jody will inspire you to take your own self-discovery tour to freedom. Her book will support you to reclaim your birthright to be seen, heard, validated, respected, honoured, treasured and loved unconditionally for who you were, who you are and who you will be.

I am proud of my friend for taking that first step… to freedom.

Susanne Calman
Wellness Consultant

www.femininespirit.com.au

Introduction

For as long as I can remember, whenever I was asked what I wanted to achieve in life or what I wanted to be when I grew up, I answered, 'to be happy'. I could never come up with anything different, or ambitious in the way that modern society expects. Now, of course, I know that happiness is not a destination that one reaches.

In addition to the desire for happiness, I always had a feeling that there was something 'more' to life. I could sense deep within that there was something greater, something with more meaning. Life had to be better, there had to be a way out of the internal unrest that I felt. I am, by nature, someone who seeks to understand the deeper meaning of life and why situations or events may occur.

Until this point in my life, there have been only a few times when I have felt as though I belonged, that I fitted in. I have felt a deep loneliness, misunderstood, unseen and like an island in a sea of people who get on with life, who are carefree, joyous and connected. I look back now and can see a couple of times when I was probably suffering from depression, including after the birth of my first child. There have been many moments when I knew with great certainty that what I was feeling was not really me, and that the feelings did not originate with me.

I have an inner strength that has allowed me to survive until now. But, underneath, deep inside, I am sensitive. Many times my core has wept, crying out for someone to take the pain away, longing for someone to hold me and tell me it will be okay. To tell me, 'you are okay'.

Eventually, the internal unrest I felt would become a tsunami that threatened to consume me. By the grace of God, a door opened and I was shown the path to walk down. With one tiny step, I began a journey that continues to this day, away from the all-consuming tsunami, towards freedom, peace and a new dawn.

I have to confess that, when that crisis point arrived, I did not love myself enough to begin this journey for me. Yes, I did not want the tsunami to consume me, but the real motivation came after I had my first child – I did not want to bring a second child into the world while I was feeling the way that I did.

The journey I embarked upon resulted in many major and life-changing decisions being made. I have said goodbye to loved ones, walked away from family, experienced faltered

Introduction

friendships and, at times, felt as though I could not bear to experience any more loss in my life. However, every decision I made came after deep and careful thought. Decisions that my heart gently whispered in moments of silence. A decision that, once made and honoured, created a sense of profound peace and knowing that I was on the right track.

I have come a long way since I began my healing journey. I have felt anger, sadness, resentment, guilt, shame, remorse and immense grief. I have released trauma. But I have also taken responsibility for the part I played in the life I was living. I am not the same woman I was when I began that journey.

This story is not about passing judgement on my family of origin or about attacking them. I feel a deep and compassionate love for all of them. I have treasured memories of a childhood in the country, shared with my siblings; of the moments I felt closest to my mum as I stood beside her in the kitchen – baking, learning and absorbing all that she had to share. We all have a story and we are all trying our best to find our way through the pain, to make sense of it and to find peace with our experiences.

This book is my way of giving meaning to the pain and suffering I've experienced. However, it's also to give meaning to the pain experienced by all of the women in my family – my ancestors – who, for various reasons, were never able to heal their suffering or have their soul song be heard (to me, a soul song is the very essence of you, your destiny). It is my way of saying this: for all that we have been through, I will step forth and make something beautiful of my life.

There are chapters in this book that were hard for me to write as they involved sharing pain that has impacted my entire family. I struggled with deciding on how much to share – out of a sense of loyalty and, I guess, a feeling that people may not believe me. But there are moments in my life that were so very pivotal and life-changing that to not include them would not do any justice to my story and my journey. I have spent so much of my life putting loyalty to others ahead of my own voice, but no more. I also feel that I need to express why I now have no relationship with most of my family of origin. If you currently have a sense of ambivalence towards your parents or family of origin or are experiencing distance from them, I hope that, by reading my story, you will be able to find peace and acceptance within yourself – without needing external validation from your family.

My journey has been about finding freedom from all that has bound me and kept me trapped. It has been about finding me, about accepting and loving me. It has been about shedding the layers that have hidden the truth of who I really am. Within this book I have included poems and paintings of mine that may be no literary masterpieces or works of art, but they were a way for me to express how I was feeling at the time.

We all deserve the opportunity to live a life where we can achieve our fullest potential, where we are free to live our truth

Introduction

in an authentic way, where we are free to let the song in our heart be heard. That is my wish for my boys, it has become my wish for myself, and it is my wish for my family and for you.

I hope my story demonstrates that pain can actually liberate us and open us up to more joy and love than we could ever imagine. Pain is a transformational tool. If we can work with it, capture its wisdom and release it (with the help of others, if need be), pain can be our friend.

Finally, I hope my story inspires you, at whatever stage of life, to know that you can overcome darkness and adversity by holding a vision for the way you want your life to look and be. For that vision to be the foundation that holds you up and drives you forward. I hope that, by taking time to let your heart whisper and guide you home, you will discover the treasure that lies within you, that has always been within you.

In order to help you with your journey of self-discovery, I have included 'For You to Ponder' questions at the end of most chapters – I invite you to journal on those questions (if you're intimidated by the thought of starting a journal, I've created a special chapter called 'The Power of Journaling: A Guide to Getting Started'). I've also included chapters such as 'For You to Delve Deeper...', which features more questions for reflection, and a 'Circle of Gratitude: Creating Your Own Ceremony' chapter. I've also created a list of resources that will enable you to explore more deeply some of the topics mentioned throughout my story.

Finding Freedom... Finding Me

May the voice that rises up from these pages ignite something within you. May you discover the treasure that lies within you. May you radiate light out into the shadows of someone else's life. And may you be the heroine in your own life who receives a standing ovation when you look back on all that you have achieved.

Jody Kalpenos
September 2015

www.jodykalpenos.com

Chapter 1

A Dam Tragedy

*'Grief is a curious thing, when it happens unexpectedly.
It is a Band-Aid being ripped
away, taking the top layer off a family.'*

~ *Jodi Picoult*

I had just turned one when my older brother Andrew drowned in a dam on a dairy farm, aged four. It was 13 May 1972, the day prior to Mother's Day here in Australia.

Two weeks before, my mother had undergone an operation to remove her gall bladder. She nearly died on the operating table. She was recovering down on a family friend's dairy farm, amongst the lush green hills of Gippsland. Andrew, my older sister and I were at the farm with her.

My dad had worked the day before Andrew's death and had stayed up all night fixing the car so that he could make the long drive down to the farm to see his family. Back then, before bypasses and freeways, the journey from my parents' place took three hours. Arriving at the farm, he had a cup of tea. Andrew came in to ask him to play. Dad was exhausted, and told Andrew he would play later, after a much-needed sleep.

Andrew took himself outside to play. My family would never see him again. Dad said it took a while to find him and it was only due to a local policeman – who had lost his own son two years prior in a dam drowning – that they began to search for him in the water. Apparently the search party looking for him was unable to get through the fence around the dam without cutting through it. The fence was quite high and they could not see any gaps. How Andrew got through, nobody knows. I have always believed that he was meant to go.

My brother's funeral was a distressing affair, according to the accounts of my aunties who were present. Both of my parents were themselves only 24 years of age and Andrew was their firstborn. How do you say goodbye to a life so young? He was the first male grandchild on my father's side, and the first on my mother's. Dad said Andrew was always happy, and in every photo I have of him, he is smiling.

My father said that Andrew's death nearly killed Opa, my Dutch grandfather, who adored him and was completely devastated. He would live long enough to see my younger brother born, three years later and three days prior to the anniversary of Andrew's death. My younger brother was actually due on the anniversary of Andrew's death but my mother requested that she be induced. Having him be born on the anniversary date would have been far too traumatic an experience for her to endure.

Another sister would be welcomed into the family 14 months after my younger brother.

The death of my brother was the first major fissure that opened up wounds in my family that would quite possibly never heal. My parents barely spoke to each other during the entire week between Andrew's death and his funeral. Dad said he just shut down. He felt guilty and blamed himself.

Andrew's death was not something that brought my parents closer together and they were definitely not united in their grief. Grief froze them and, in particular, I feel that it froze my mother, resulting in the creation of a permanent barrier that I've never really penetrated. I cannot judge her for it; it is what it is, and she was a mother who had lost her baby. Only two weeks earlier, she herself had nearly died. With two young children still alive, life had to go on.

My parents did not go to counselling because mum said she did not need to go. I suppose counselling was not as commonplace as it is now. My sister and I were not permitted to speak Andrew's name, an impossible task when I was only one and she was three. Andrew was my sister's idol. They were very close in age and they went everywhere together. I cannot imagine the level of loss and devastation she must have felt.

As far as I'm aware, my mother never returned to Andrew's grave. I had always thought that my father had also never returned to the grave, but recently I asked him if he had. He told me that he visited him many times and that he still sometimes did in his mind. He did not want 'the little fella' to think he was forgotten. Dad also said he had made a plaque for the grave but it was not a long-lasting one. He never got back there to fix it and my mum always refused to go. When he told me this, I sobbed, as I had always felt that my brother had been neglected and abandoned.

Andrew's death hung over our family like an ever-present heavy, grey and sombre cloud that created a layer of darkness that would never lift. He was never forgotten but he was also not really talked about. In writing this chapter, I realised that I had never sat down and asked my dad anything about that day, what followed or what Andrew was like. I was always concerned that my dad would be too upset to talk about it. Recently I finally plucked up the courage, and asked him. He was happy to share his memories and I trusted my intuition in knowing the moments when I was not to pursue any further. The pain of losing Andrew was still evident within him but, equally, the love and joy in knowing Andrew for just four short years radiated from his eyes and his face.

Even though I have always known that the cloud hung over our family, I was surprised when my mum handed me some writing I had done at school at the age of eight – writing that revealed how aware I was of Andrew's presence and his death's lasting effect on the family. Overlooking the error in the timing

A Dam Tragedy

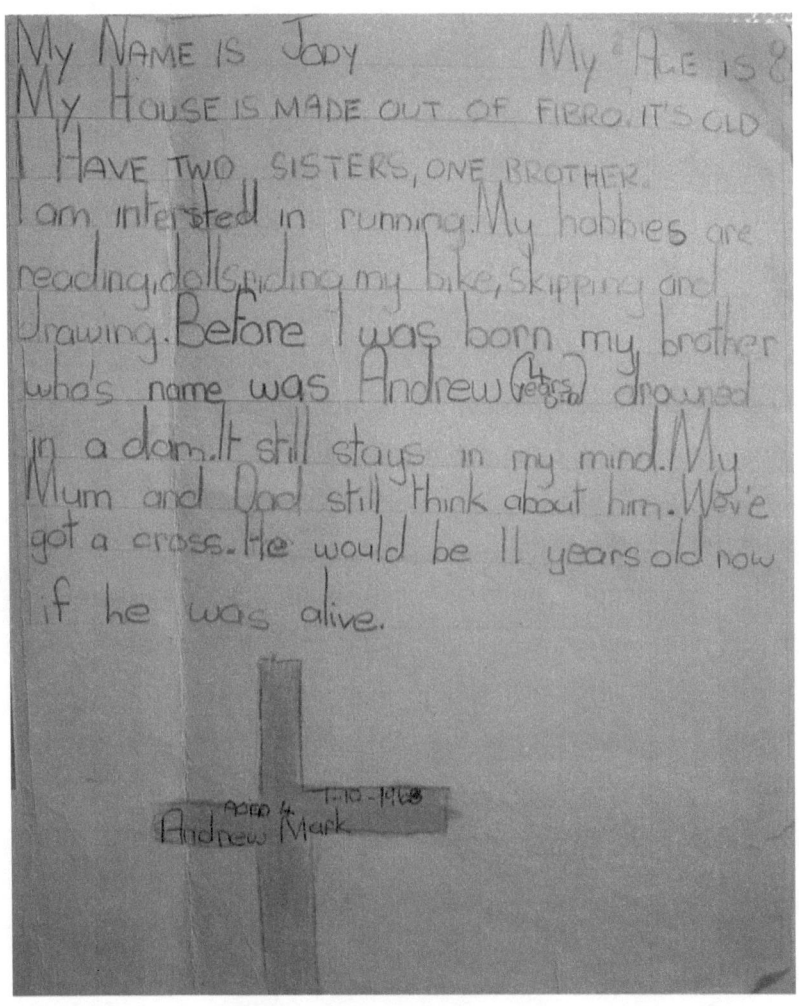

An understanding of my family's grief, at eight years of age...

of his death (it was not before I was born), I found that reading this made me feel incredibly sad.

Grief is a very personal thing and I cannot imagine the pain and trauma that my parents experienced at that time. I believe that the burden of guilt and the feelings of blame, anger and loss, which they have carried for 43 years, had a huge impact on their lives, and this subsequently affected me. As a surviving child, a baby, who needed love and nurturing but whose parents were not fully available, the aftershock of Andrew dying rippled out across the years and left behind fractures and piles of rubble, wounding, blocking and crippling me.

It was from that time that I learned how to stuff my emotions deep inside. I would go on to become a master practitioner of denying my feelings and leaving them unexpressed. I had been marked with the pattern of generations, a pattern whereby feelings were not embraced, and where it was natural not to talk about how one was feeling or what effect another's actions had on you. I would be loyal to that blueprint until I became a mother myself.

For You to Ponder

In the 'For You to Ponder' sections at the end of most chapters, I invite you to journal on the questions contained within (if you're unfamiliar with the process of journaling, see my 'The Power of Journaling: A Guide to Getting Started' chapter later in this book).

- Do you remember the dreams and hopes of the eight-year-old girl you once were? If you can, write out your list…

- Has there been a death in your family, with the effects of that death rippling out across the years? If so, what effects can you identify?

- Can you identify patterns in your family of origin that have been passed down the generations?

- Is there one particular pattern that you recognise in yourself that you could start to work on breaking? A pattern that you can see is not for your highest good? A pattern that is harmful to you in some way, or that holds you back from living life to the fullest expression of your truth? The very act of identifying and becoming conscious of any patterns, along with writing in your journal, begins the healing process. The path taken to heal these patterns will be different for everyone – there is no right or wrong way. Just know that there are deeper tools available to you. Be open to how this healing may occur. People and resources will then cross your path to assist you.

Chapter 2
Running Free

'I am living breathing freedom.'

~ Hiroko Sakai

The city of Melbourne, Australia, is my home. I love the underlying European culture, and being in close proximity to the fresh food markets, the cafés and the beaches. I love that I can be invisible, if I choose to be. However, my childhood was spent encased in nature's embrace and at times I yearn for the fresh air, silence, space and simplicity of life in the country.

I grew up on a large block of land in the village of Macedon, north of Melbourne. Back then, there was no dual-lane freeway and the city bustle seemed far away. City lights did not obscure the night sky, so the vastness and beauty of the Milky Way above was sparkling clear. In summer, the land would cool down at night and a gentle breeze would enter through open windows, bringing relief and making it possible to sleep on those hottest of Australian summer nights.

We had a large vegetable garden, chickens, dogs and cats, and a rabbit, a lamb and a duck. There was an old Fiat parked

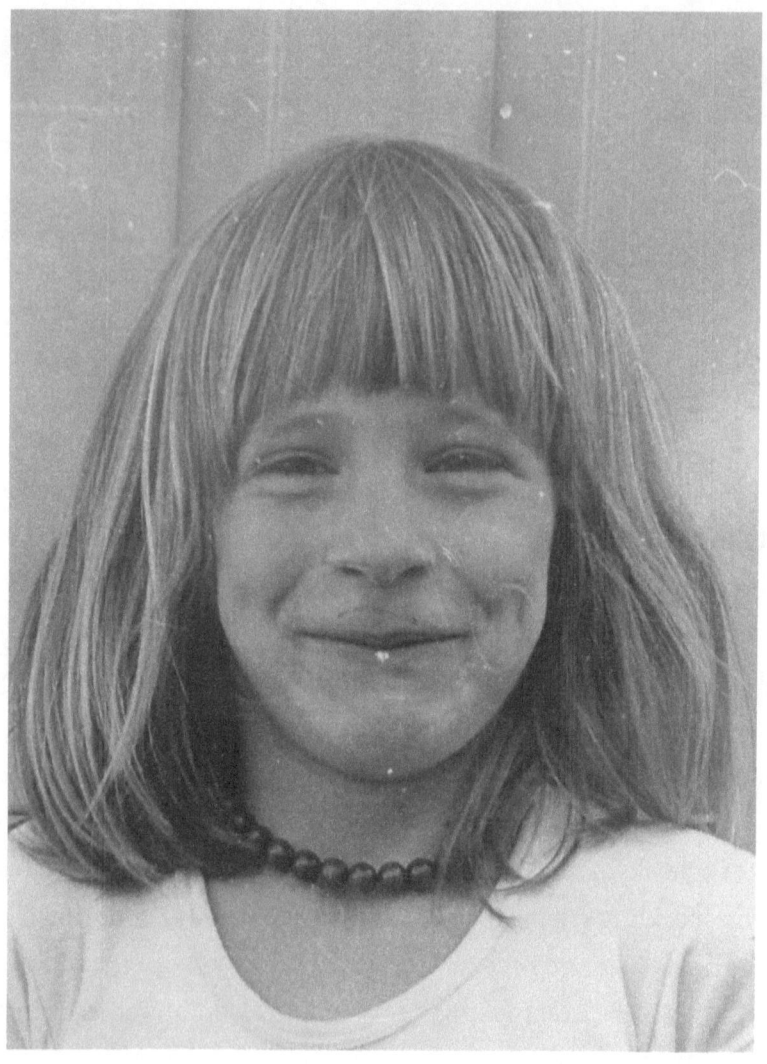

Me, aged eight

behind the chook shed, and a cubby house that we used to love playing in. A large Hills Hoist clothesline was perfect for the washing that a family of six produced. When our pet duck chased me, quacking angrily, the clothesline was a great place on which to climb on top as I tried to escape, screaming for my mum to rescue me.

The block next to us was filled with large deep-green Cyprus trees and small pine-tree saplings. We had our own mini enchanted forest. There were also large gum trees that had fallen many years before and had become covered in moss – trees that were perfect for climbing over and hiding under. The trees and forest were an ideal place for fairytale red and orange toadstools to flourish, although we always knew not to touch them. The ground was covered in pine needles and the smell of pine would fill our nostrils as we acted out our adventures.

Large gum trees and bush were all around us. This was our playground. A place for us to roam and explore, unhindered by rules and regulations. With a small house and four growing children, the outdoors was the natural place for us to spend our time.

On hot summer days, we would put on our gumboots, grab our empty ice-cream containers and walk to the rambling blackberry bushes behind our block, bushes that were untouched by any poison. Stomping our feet on the ground to let snakes know we were coming, we would begin picking the luscious black berries, their flesh warm from the sun – some making it into the container; the sweetest and juiciest ones going no further than our hungry mouths.

With our arms and legs bearing scratches from the blackberry thorns and with lips and fingers stained purple, we would deliver the harvest to Mum, who proceeded to turn it into blackberry jam, dessert for the evening or some other sweet treat.

In winter, we sometimes woke up to snow on the ground. Because of the cold and the damp, it was time to create our fun inside. We rarely watched television, and reading was my favourite indoor pastime. Books enabled me to go to another world; they opened my imagination, showed me a place beyond that which I knew. Many a night I would be under my covers with my bedside lamp on, reading an Enid Blyton book, savouring the words and the adventures of *The Magic Faraway Tree*. If there is one thing I could do, even now, to nourish my soul on a regular basis, it would be to spend a day with my head in a book, preferably with the sound of rain falling on a tin roof. Simple joys.

Because we lived out of town, gas was not connected to our property. Our house had a wood stove, and its warmth meant it was the first place we'd go to stand, leaning against it, letting it take the chill away. I was blessed to be brought up with a bountiful vegetable garden, fresh eggs, homemade jams, sauces, biscuits, slices and cakes, not to mention hearty soups and stews that sat bubbling away on top of the wood stove. I loved standing beside my mother in the kitchen, helping her to bake, in the hope that I would get to lick the beaters or the bowl! On those rare days when Mum made vanilla slice I could be found right beside her, as custard was, and still is, one of my all-time favourite sweets. I did not taste a bought biscuit until my teens and normal tomato sauce is still something I am getting used to. There is something so deeply nourishing and comforting about walking into a house and breathing in the smell of oven-baked goodies – that aroma creates a sense of 'home' for me.

My happiest memories from childhood are those that involved us playing and walking in the bush, climbing over those fallen-down trees, finding the red and orange toadstools, picking and eating those large, juicy blackberries, running under the sprinkler, playing cricket, collecting firewood in the forest with dad, playing 'spotlight' in the dark with our cousins and just being free.

There were some things I did not enjoy, such as the jumping jack ants whose stinging bite would make my foot swell to twice its size, and the chilblains that would appear in winter, causing areas of my fingers and toes to become hot and itchy.

I recall seeing kangaroos feeding on the dewy grass early in the morning, the laugh of kookaburras piercing the stillness, the call of a magpie, and looking up and seeing koalas sitting in the gum trees out the front of our house. I also remember climbing small pine-tree saplings, swinging on them back and forth – the swinging was a whole lot of fun until the day my tree broke and I fell down to the ground, somehow avoiding breaking any bones!

Before I was a teen, my childhood was played out on nature's canvas. I loved growing up immersed in nature, our play activities changing according to the seasons. Our lungs always filled with fresh clean air, our bodies fit and cheeks rosy. I am grateful that my parents chose to live in the country, for that kind of freedom is impossible to buy. I feel incredibly blessed for having that as my foundation and, to this day, the country calls to me when the city begins to swallow my spirit.

However, when I was 11 everything changed and never again would I truly run free.

For You to Ponder

- What are some of your favourite memories from childhood? Can you recall sights, tastes, smells and sounds?

- What skills or other things did you learn from your mother or father? (My father taught me how to change a tyre, check the oil in my car, hammer a nail and chop wood.)

- What were some of the games or hobbies you enjoyed as a child? Have you lost your connection with these?

Chapter 3
The Flame of Terror

'There are wounds that never show on the body that are deeper and more hurtful than anything that bleeds.'

~ Laurell K Hamilton

The date 7 February 2009 will forever be remembered in Australia as Black Saturday. A day when the land would be scorched so badly that it resembled a nuclear wasteland, when too many human and animal lives were lost, when homes filled with a lifetime of memories would be extinguished from the landscape. A day that was, to those of us who experienced Ash Wednesday many years before, eerily familiar.

It was through my adult eyes and other senses that I experienced Black Saturday 2009. However, when I awoke the following day, a little girl was standing in my lounge room, her heart filled with terror, her eyes weeping unshed tears from long ago, her grief surfacing from deep within, the emotional wounds raw as she watched images on television from the fire-affected areas – in particular, an image of a little boy in a 4WD, trembling with fear and mumbling incoherently, cut to my very core. In that moment

I saw myself. A little girl, a survivor of Ash Wednesday who had lost everything, who was visited by terror and who now wished with all her heart that this little boy had been spared the same fate.

I awoke on the morning of Wednesday 16 February 1983; I was 11 years of age and had just started secondary school in Kyneton, a town 20 minutes away. It was the last day of life as I knew it.

From the moment I awoke, the day felt different. The energy was unsettling, the heat already rising fast, the wind making its presence felt early. Deep inside my body a feeling of foreboding began to stir. The sense of eeriness increased as the day passed, the temperature soared into the 40s and the wind became dry and unpleasant. Fear formed in the pit of my stomach, joining forces with the feeling of foreboding – so much so that I began to feel sick.

As I sat in the classroom staring out of the windows, my fear was fed by the view that greeted me across the fields towards Woodend and the Wombat State Forest. The horizon had turned brown. The rumour was that it was due to dust storms. My friend and I were talking and our instincts told us that it was no dust storm. The view of the horizon was mesmerising – you didn't want to take your eyes away from it, afraid that if you did you would miss something vitally important.

On the bus that afternoon, I was very anxious to get home and be with Mum. However, when we stopped in Woodend as per normal to let off students, the bus drivers who had arrived in town left their buses and gathered in a huddle with concerned expressions on their faces. We did not move for what seemed like a very long time and my fear began to take away my ability to speak. We did not know what was going on, but whispers started that there was a fire and they were deciding whether or not to take the buses any further. This was in the era before mobile phones, so there was no way of contacting our parents.

Eventually, our bus headed off and we were dropped at our normal stop near our home. On this day, however, Mum met us there, which was something she never did. We were almost an hour late in getting home and she was extremely anxious. There were helicopters flying overhead, their presence a sign of something sinister in the air. Most tellingly of all was the absence of any sound from the animals or birds. Apart from the wind, nature was silent. Nature knew, the animals and birds knew. Experiencing that silence is hard to convey in words, but I'll never forget how it felt.

Mum informed us that a fire had started in East Trentham and was burning in the Wombat State Forest. The concern was that when a predicted south-westerly change came through that evening, the fire would head towards Macedon and Mount Macedon. So began the waiting game.

The hours that followed were spent in preparation. Taking washing off the line, packing our school uniforms, choosing what personal items we wanted to take with us, putting our chosen things in the car. I selected a big soft toy that I had received the previous Christmas, and my collection of Enid Blyton books. We were not permitted to take many things, as there were six of us as well as the pet dogs, canaries and the one cat we could find. At the back of house was a bungalow where my sisters and I usually slept, and I can still picture myself leaving it, closing the door for one last time.

At 6 o'clock, I joined Mum as she drove to Gisborne to get fish and chips for dinner. It was too hot for her to put on the wood stove to make dinner, and a total fire ban day meant no barbecues. That drive, which took only 10 minutes, was terribly eerie. Not a soul to be seen anywhere. The roads were empty, the streets deserted. What on earth was coming?

As darkness descended, the forecast change had started to come through. Now the aroma of a burning forest was reaching our nostrils, with the smoke catching in our throats and ash floating down upon us. A rumble was building that sounded like the roar of 100 jumbo jets flying overhead, except that the roar was heading towards us, closer and closer. One of my parents made a futile attempt to hose down the house, causing the outside lights to blow and leaving the crushing oppression of darkness to fall upon us. Shortly afterwards the power went off, rendering the fire pump useless. The monster was making its ominous presence felt.

Sometime around 9.30pm we received a frantic phone call from Mum's best friend, a CFA volunteer, who had been keeping us informed all night as she listened to the CB radio. She told us that we had to go; the fire was charging towards us, it was near her house and, as the crow flies through the bush, it was almost on our doorstep. Somehow, my parents managed to get the dogs, canaries and one cat into the two cars, along with me and my siblings (our few belongings having been packed earlier), all while frantically running around. The other cat could not be found – although, thankfully, we found him a few days later, singed but alive.

I recall sitting in the station wagon, looking out of the back window, wondering what Mum and Dad were doing, when all of a sudden the fire appeared on the edge of the forest behind us. A huge ball of panic rose up in me; sheer terror began coursing through every fibre of my being. I screamed over and over, 'let's go, let's go,' suddenly realising that my dad (with my brother and older sister) had driven off down to our elderly neighbours. Mum joined me, my younger sister and the canaries in the station wagon. We sat there waiting for Dad to return. The advancing flames were threatening, closing in. I thought I was going to die. I thought I would be burnt alive.

Suddenly, my dad drove up the laneway. Mum pulled out and followed him, and at 10pm we finally fled our house, literally driving just ahead of the firestorm. So began a four-hour journey to find a place to stay where we would be safe. The town pub was full; a grassfire at Riddells Creek had us changing direction. Looking back towards Mount Macedon as we drove into Gisborne, the night sky was lit up by an orange glow – the mountain was ablaze. We arrived in Diggers Rest to find our friends' house already full, so our parents kept going, driving us towards my auntie's house in Corio, the smoke from the Great Ocean Road fires making us feel as if we would never escape this nightmare. Finally, at 2am, wide-eyed, exhausted, terrified and thirsty, we fell into the welcoming embrace of my aunt and grandma. Everyone had scorched throats from the smoke, except for Dad, who had taken along a couple of beers for the drive (this being a time when drink-driving laws were not as tough as they are now). Mum had rung ahead from Diggers Rest, so beds were waiting for us. Out of sheer exhaustion, we collapsed onto them and fell asleep.

We awoke the next morning to find that Mum and Dad, along with my aunt and uncle, had already headed off back to our property to see what was left. Mum had not slept, having listened to the radio, hoping for the good news that would never come. Grandma stayed with us, trying her best to comfort us, but, really, what could she say or do? I wandered like a lost soul around the backyard, waiting for my parents' return. I was traumatised. All I wanted was my parents. I needed my parents. I needed their presence and their love so that I could feel, despite everything, that I was secure. They were gone for the whole day, searching for friends, checking up on the whereabouts of others and witnessing the landscape, which was now a wasteland. Their return did not bring with it comfort, nurturing or the sense of security I so desperately needed. The shock, trauma and exhaustion that the last 24 hours had delivered meant they couldn't support me in the way that I needed supporting. However, I cannot imagine how my parents felt, as they had made such a difficult journey that day – nor can I imagine what it took out of them to get us all out alive, and to safety.

They informed us that everything was gone. Our elderly neighbour had bravely walked his beloved Shetland ponies into town and I am sure that only by the grace of God did he make it there safely ahead of the fire. He would spend the night outside the pub, with CFA firemen above him on the roof keeping 300 townspeople safe, never leaving the side of his ponies, watching the town go up in flames. His wife would make it over the top of Mount Macedon before the fire front decimated the mountain but there were many anxious hours before each would learn that the other had survived. Their bluestone house was the only one to survive in our little pocket, and, in an ironic and cruel twist, his wife would lose her life in a house fire over 20 years later.

At my aunt's house, we would find laughter amongst the tears at some of the things we had saved from our home. My little sister, who was seven at the time, had packed all of the house and shed keys – these were no longer of any use, of course, but it was good thinking, regardless! She had also packed all of the cordial bottles and a jar of peanut butter (her favourite spread at the time).

A week later, my aunt and uncle drove my siblings and I up to see our property. I was in the front seat, beside my aunt, and as we drew closer to home, I grabbed her hand, not really ready at the age of 11 to confront what I was about to see. The trees were black, some had fallen down and the ground was scorched and bare. Where houses once stood, there were gaping holes. Chimneys, the only things left, stood to attention. I walked around the remains of our home by myself, tears flowing, my heart breaking. The first 11 years of my life now a pile of black and grey ash. It was too much to take in. My aunt held me in a warm embrace as she allowed me to weep for my loss, to shed tears of terror that had been held in for a week. Her love would be the only comfort and nurturing I received that day.

We would find out later that the local policeman had been trapped on a road opposite where our house was located, and he recounted how our house had exploded. The gas bottle installed for additional heating had blasted our little fibro house apart. This would explain why our parents would find pieces of our house scattered metres from where it had stood. Working out the timing, it seemed that we had left a mere 10 minutes before this explosion. If ever there was a time to thank God, this was it.

'A Child's Terror'

Fire, heat, darkness, night,
Heart thumping, stomach tight.

Eyes wide, fear gripping,
What is coming? Ash dripping.

The noise, the roar, terror rising,
Smoke choking, flames arriving.

Screams, panic, please, please go,
Will we make it, I do not know.

Sleep, rest, a long way away,
Safety won't come for another day.

Our house all gone, our life a mess,
Tears and suffering stain my dress.

One so young should not know,
Such trauma, pain and deep sorrow.

For years the terror and pain remained,
Innocence and love never regained.

Ash Wednesday is and will always be,
A day etched deep within my memory.

I have carried that trauma within me ever since. However, in the last three years, with all of the healing that I've done, its effect has diminished. Although, I must admit that writing all of this down, and reliving some of the moments of sheer terror, has triggered more tears. On hot and windy days, my heart tightens and my stomach swirls. My nose can sniff out bushfire smoke before anyone else can, and dreams of fire return to haunt me every summer. Thankfully, these have almost disappeared now. When I close my eyes I am transported back as if it were yesterday.

So, yes, whenever I think of that little boy in the 4WD on Black Saturday, I reach out to him through my heart and soul as someone who experienced the same terror and trauma. I feel a connection borne of shared experience and I know there will be many more who will join in this – for such is the nature of the Australian bush in the heat of summer.

Ash Wednesday would mark another point in time for our family when life really was never the same again.

Chapter 4

A Deep Chasm Opens Up

'After all, when a stone is dropped into a pond, the water continues quivering even after the stone has sunk to the bottom.'

~ Arthur Golden

For the two weeks following the fire, our family was separated. My sisters stayed with my aunt in Corio, while I, having begged and pleaded with my parents, remained with them and my brother in a caravan on our property. During this time I took on the responsibility of cooking some meals and helping where I could. I comforted my father who sat sobbing one day, heartbroken that he had not saved our chickens. I accompanied my mother as we exchanged vouchers and coupons for tools and basic supplies. At the age of 11, I felt that I had taken on the responsibility of an adult within my family, and this was a pattern that would be repeated many times over. We did not attend any school for those two weeks.

When my parents were lent a second caravan, the family was reunited and we returned to the semblance of a normal routine, going back to school and our sporting activities. My high school provided a space for the children of families affected to do our homework once a week, feeding us dinner and driving us home.

We stayed home from school to watch the remains of our house being scooped up and dumped into the back of a tip truck. From memory, it took only three or four trucks to remove it all and leave behind a clean, flat empty canvas. A surreal experience, seeing all your belongings and the house in which you had grown up reduced to waste, good for nothing and nobody except to become lost in the vastness of a rubbish tip.

After the fires we talked about 'life before' and 'life after'. In the months following we would look for a toy or something else and then realise, 'oh, that's right, that burnt in the fire'. No more would we roam in the forest, most of it having been cleared as it was deemed unsafe. Other families moved in where the pine trees and blackberries once stood.

My parents chose to build a kit home, with the hope that it would be completed before the winter set in. They would be dealt a blow when the company building the home went bankrupt. The house was not complete, my parents had paid most of their insurance money to the building company and they only had a very small amount left (which was also needed to purchase furnishings) – they had only had insurance for the house itself and therefore received no money for the contents lost.

A Deep Chasm Opens Up

Fortunately, two builders originally employed by the building company had become good friends, and agreed to stay on and finish off the house. My parents took over some of the work that needed to be done, with my mother painting long into the night after we were in bed, my father working every spare hour (outside of his normal job) to get our house finished. We moved in a little behind schedule but before the real chill of winter set in.

It transpired that the building company had defrauded Mum and Dad and a few other people, taking advantage of everyone's vulnerability after the fire. A court case ensued and my father was a key witness. The stress of the fire, the building of the house and now the court case triggered a disease in him that doctors believe had lain dormant in his body since his early teens.

On a cold and wintry afternoon in June 1984, we walked into the house after school to be told bluntly by our mother that our father, at the age of 36, had been diagnosed with multiple sclerosis (MS). My dad sat in the corner, looking as though he had done something wrong, and I felt in that moment that my mum was angry with him. I had netball training to go to that night but I could not focus when I was there – my mind was racing, filled with unanswered questions, frightened about what this news meant for us, for our future and for him. Would we get the disease? Was he going to die? What was going to change?

My father's illness had a huge impact on our family. He was angry and bitter. His feeling was, 'Why me?'. He was young and active and had a sharp, intelligent mind. He had a long life ahead of him. Soon, the effects of the disease meant that he had to give up riding his beloved motorbike to work. Then, as the effects worsened he had to give up work; his double vision meant it was no longer safe for him to drive. I watched my father become someone I did not recognise and I became angry, too. Why was he not fighting it? Why was he just feeling sorry for himself? Why?

With the benefit of many years of reflection I realise that it must have been very hard for him to come to terms with his illness at such a young age, and so soon after losing the house and going through the court case. I know now what it feels like to have so many emotional events piled onto you in such a short space of time. He was also the provider of a family of six. When did he have time to process all that had happened? To me, his diagnosis was the final incident in a string of traumatic events that raised his stress levels to a point where the disease was triggered into action.

My teenage years were characterised by the tension that existed within our home. I lived with parents who, from my observations, were struggling, angry at what life had dealt them, trying to parent children who were in the most challenging years of their lives. Everything was triggered. I felt powerless, with little control over what was happening around me.

A Deep Chasm Opens Up

I found solace on the netball court, training and playing most days of the week. It was the place I could go and forget about home, pushing my body further, channelling my feelings into each and every game and every throw of the ball. It was the only thing that I felt I had control over – my fitness, my skill level, my performance. I loved it and relied on it for my sanity. Looking back, I truly believe that netball was the only thing that saved me from imploding and sinking into depression.

As a family we began to grow apart, never really coming back together, only ever achieving a sense of togetherness for small moments. Even then it often felt that we were simply doing our duty. We never sat down together and talked about our feelings. Everything was bottled up and left unsaid. There was silence at the dinner table, something I hated. I continued to suppress everything, to stifle my cries, to leave my wounds gaping and bleeding because, well, what was the point? I felt that no one was willing to listen anyway, and if I did say something I was told to put it into perspective and 'get on with it'.

My siblings and I did attend counselling after the fire, a service that had been provided to all victims. From memory, we talked more about the death of my brother and the effect of that on the family than we did about the fire. I told no one at school that I was attending these sessions, even though I would disappear regularly for the day, as we had to travel to the Royal Children's Hospital in Melbourne. I would tell only one friend about my dad's diagnosis. Perhaps I felt ashamed, or perhaps I simply could not talk about it for fear of the emotion overwhelming me.

I managed to complete my final year of high school, gaining my Higher School Certificate despite failing maths; for some reason, in my final year, after being an A-grade student in two mathematics subjects for six years, I lost all confidence in my mathematics ability. I could not get it together, despite using the money I earnt at the local supermarket to pay for a tutor. He told me I did not need him, that I knew the answers. However, I finished the year on a mark of 34%. To this day I have never recovered confidence in my ability to do maths, nor have I ever understood what happened in my mind that saw me plummet from an A to an F so quickly.

Regardless, I was accepted into university, deferring for a year to work, and to save for my own car. I chose to work full time at the local supermarket where I had been working on a casual basis. My theory was that after 12 months I would not be tempted to give up my place at university, and that theory worked. I saved hard and achieved my goal of paying for my first car. In the year I was to turn 19 I left my home town in the country and moved to Melbourne. Although I cried on the first night away from my parents, I loved having distance from all the drama and heavy emotions that pervaded the family home.

A Deep Chasm Opens Up

In six short years, a deep and ravenous chasm had opened up in my family. The fire had been the catalyst and the dominoes had fallen one by one from then on. There were times when I thought that I would lose myself in that chasm, but I look back now and see that I was never alone, I had Spirit guiding me and bringing to me the people who would keep me from falling in. Teachers, coaches, employers and guidance that came in many other different forms, giving me a reason to hope that something better lay ahead. My relationship with my father would be fractured, almost beyond repair. The impact of those six years would take many, many years to unravel and some parts may be beyond fixing.

For You to Ponder

- Has someone in your family ever been diagnosed with a serious illness? If so, how has it affected you?

- Can you identify characters in your teenage or school years who inspired you, believed in you or guided you on your journey? I invite you to journal on how they helped you, and to express gratitude for their contribution.

Chapter 5

The Wider World Calls to Me

'... travel is more than the seeing of sights; it is a change that goes on, deep and permanent, in the ideas of living.'

~ Miriam Beard

Moving to Melbourne in early January of 1990 (at the age of 18), in preparation for university, marked the beginning of a long and happy period in my life.

I met new people from various backgrounds and my friendship circle grew. I ate way too much melted cheese on toast and danced till 5am, losing myself in the music of the '60s, '70s and '80s. I was always happy to be the 'designated driver' on nights out, content with drinking water and Coca-Cola, my sole mission to express my emotions on the dance floor. Music is and has always been the one thing guaranteed to reach deep within and touch the part of me where I bottle up my emotions.

In 1994, an opportunity arose for me to move to Sydney. I did not spend long thinking about it, knowing that it was the right step to take, feeling that the move would put more distance between my family and myself. Luckily for me, the company I was working for transferred me. For the next five years I made my home in Sydney on the leafy North Shore. Wherever I live, I seek out a leafy and green place to reside – doing so makes me feel a little connected to the 'country' that runs through my veins.

I was very much a tourist while living in Sydney, never tiring of the view from the bus as it hurtled across the Harbour Bridge. Locals would have their heads down, missing the colours of the morning sky, the glistening of the sun on the water below and the view of the boats and ferries taking workers to the city for the day. Friends introduced me to foods I had never tasted, including laksa, and Japanese and Vietnamese foods. My tastebuds were truly awakened.

Work overtook my life and, when I look back now, I see that – just as netball did for me in my teens – work was the gate holding back my internal floodwaters. I would learn in the next few years that hiding yourself away for 60 to 80 hours a week in an office, with little social life, does not make the inner pain disappear – nor does moving halfway around the world. You can run but you cannot hide. Always, always, the pain will catch up with you in the form of illness or in how your external life is created.

I had some memorable times with the people I worked with, in both Melbourne and Sydney. We shared lots of laughter and tears, bonded during highly stressful times on the job and probably drank way too much red wine and coffee. It was in the days when long lunches were tolerated. If you worked long hours your employer made it up to you in other ways, and Friday night drinks were legendary. I found love and lost love and the people I worked with were like family to me. They are memories that I treasure, and I made some life-long friends who have stuck with me despite the distance and passing of time. These friends are important to me, as they are the only ones remaining who know Jody as a woman – before I became a wife and mother.

Then, in 1999, at the age of 28, having resigned from my job and packed up my life, I flew out to Athens via London to meet up with the boyfriend who would become my husband five years later. My boyfriend was from Sydney and we worked for the same company – I actually hired him as I was in charge of recruitment at the time! He had left work seven months earlier to work and travel overseas. I made the decision to join him in Greece and then to go and live and work in London.

My world was expanding even more and I was elated. For as long as I could remember I had been drawn to anyone who was from overseas. I would attach myself to them, soak up their accent, ask about where they lived, and enjoy tasting the cuisine of their country. Now, I was able to live in and travel to places that I had long dreamed of. My auntie would tell me later that she was thrilled that I had made this decision, for I had talked about travelling since the age of 12.

Finding Freedom... Finding Me

I was fortunate to spend three months in Greece, where my boyfriend's father was from. We stayed with family in Athens, and although we did not speak Greek nor they English we somehow got by. By day we would walk into the city of Athens, wandering amongst the ruins, around the museums and the Plaka, no time restrictions dictating how our day unfolded. However, I never got used to the noise of the hundreds of motorbikes that would take off as the traffic lights turned green, the rumble splintering my nervous system each time.

After three weeks in Athens, we were taken to a house in a small village on the Peloponnese peninsula, where we stayed for four weeks on our own. The house was basic, with no television or radio. To use the kettle you had to turn off all the other electricity. Having a shower was a life and death matter as the water was heated directly above you through a power unit. Orange and lemon trees filled the backyard, their branches heavy with the ripe fruit – a permanent supply of fresh orange juice on hand just outside the back door.

We had arrived in Greece at the end of winter, March 1999, and at the time of the Bosnian War. There were no English newspapers around and we relied on a weekly phone call from family to keep us informed. On a few occasions, our nerves were jangled as fighter jets flew overhead. Apart from some concerns about the war, our days were spent sleeping in, sitting in the sun reading, and walking down the hill to a village beside the

Marmara Sea, where we would sometimes treat ourselves to lunch, and at other times buy supplies. It was the perfect place to rest and recover from too many years of working too many long hours. The simplicity of it all was in such contrast to the frenetic pace of living in Sydney and I melted into it, allowing it to permeate and cleanse my tired mind and body.

On Easter Saturday we were picked up by my boyfriend's uncle and cousin and driven to the village of Oasis. It is a tiny village with a beautiful view down the valley towards the Marmara Sea and the snow-capped mountains of Central Greece. We would stay for three days and meet more family, including my boyfriend's grandfather, Pappous, whose mode of transport around the village and surrounding hills was a donkey. Experiencing a traditional Greek Easter with family was memorable. Walking through the kitchen of Uncle John's house, my boyfriend told me not to look to the left, which, of course, I did. There, hanging upside down, was a freshly killed lamb, bleeding out to be ready for cooking the next day. A slap of reality about life in a rural Greek village!

We watched as Pappous prepared his voice for midnight mass by drinking honey and chamomile tea. At 11pm we walked down the dirt road to the small village church, my boyfriend escorted up the front while I stayed down the back with the women and children. It was an emotional mass as Pappous sang some of the service and my boyfriend's uncle presided as a newly ordained Greek Orthodox priest. On the stroke of midnight, everyone went outside and circled the church three times, the local men shot their guns into the air and afterwards everyone returned home to partake of the traditional post-mass feast.

Waking late on Easter Sunday to the aroma of the lamb already cooking slowly on the spit, we spent the morning relaxing, amused as the sound of gunfire echoed through the valleys. Neighbours seemingly 'talked' to each other through gunfire messages, and we watched nervously as Pappous (who was in his 90s) had a go at shooting the shotgun, his shoulder lurching backwards but his tiny frame, strong from a life on the farm, standing firm. I made sure I was behind him – just in case!

I had so many wonderful experiences during my time in Greece – amazing, simple, home-cooked Greek food, family moments to be treasured… and an experience of how you can connect with another person even when the language you speak is foreign to the other. Everyone shares a common language of the heart, and the eyes tell you so much of what is not understood by the ears.

My boyfriend's father, mother and aunt spent a few weeks visiting their family in Greece, and I will never forget standing at Athens airport as we said goodbye to them before they left to return to Australia. It was the first time in 37 years that his aunt had been home to Greece after emigrating to Australia. I was with Pappous, whose eyes filled with tears at the sight of his daughter leaving once again. I looked at him and I felt his sadness, his loss and the knowledge that he may never see her again (which he did not). I nodded my understanding and embraced him, my own tears starting to fall, my heart aching with his.

As the weeks passed by, spring arrived and the Peloponnese came alive. The beauty of the cherry trees, their pink blossoms softening the ruins of Ancient Olympia, and the wild flowers that bloomed across the countryside… all were signs that the land was awakening from the cold of winter. Restaurant owners were slowly opening up after closing for the colder months, painting and freshening up their places ready for the onslaught of tourists to come. It was time for us to move on and our destination of choice was the Greek islands.

Joined by my boyfriend's brother, we headed off with our backpacks onto the ferries and began a four-week journey around some of the islands. We chose Paros, Mykonos, Delos, Santorini and Rhodes. A carefree time of playing the tourist, sipping on Nescafé frappés to pass the time, enjoying long lunches, sitting in the sun, watching the sunset and soaking up history that emanated from every corner. The only time constraint we had was the ferry timetable; being early in the season, ferries were not running as often. We were able to find fantastic places to stay that would treble in price a few weeks later, never planning ahead but negotiating on the pier with eager landlords as we arrived at each new destination.

I loved the mosaics on Delos; the vibrant red and pink colours of the bougainvillea in stark contrast to the whitewashed houses on Mykonos; the best gyros I have ever tasted on Paros; the history and architecture in the old town of Rhodes; and, of course, the famous sunsets and caldera of Santorini.

Our tourist visas and money were running out, and even though we had not managed to see all that we had planned, it was time to make our way to London, where we were going to live and work.

My time in Greece really did provide me with treasured memories for life. I was welcomed into my boyfriend's family, my mind expanded with history and knowledge, I experienced living without time constraints for the first time in my life and I ate simple, fresh and delicious Greek food that has never truly been re-created for me elsewhere. It was also the place where I altered forever my views on working long hours unnecessarily. I had realised how futile it had been and I vowed never to lose myself like that again.

For You to Ponder

- Are you in any way trying to run away from inner pain? If you are, can you see how this is showing up in your life – in the form of illness, in your relationships, in your work or in your general day-to-day life?

- How many hours per week are you working at the moment? Are you working long hours with little social life? If you are working long hours, are you happy – deep within yourself – to continue to do so?

- Have you lost yourself in your work (now or previously), and become a slave to a corporation? Do you have a sense of work–life balance?

Chapter 6

Big Ben, Baguettes & Bananas

'Twenty years from now you will be more disappointed by the things you didn't do than by the ones you did do. So throw off the bowlines. Sail away from the safe harbour. Catch the trade winds in your sails. Explore. Dream. Discover.'

~ Mark Twain

It was June 1999, the beginning of summer in London and the start of the next chapter of our adventure. I had to pinch myself to believe that I was really there; a simple country girl who had long dreamed of faraway lands was about to set up a home and live like a local in a city with such a long and rich history.

Fortunately, I had a friend who lived in Battersea at the time, and she kindly allowed us to stay with her while we set up all of the necessary paperwork and found ourselves a place to live. Our early days were filled with looking for a job, setting up bank accounts, registering for the National Health Service (NHS) and navigating our way around the rental market.

We could not believe the state of some of the rental places that were advertised. We were beginning to despair until we spied an ad for a rental in an area we had not considered. It was near two tube stations (Oval and Vauxhall), in a four-level Victorian terrace that had been turned into four flats, each one occupying a level of the terrace. It was fully furnished, had access to a pretty little garden at the back and was on the ground floor. To make us feel at home, it was directly opposite the Oval cricket ground and we looked out of our lounge room bay window at a huge Foster's beer sign. We found that hilarious and loved the place.

We moved our backpacks in and collected some boxes that I had had shipped over. We settled into our new home, and I found a temporary job just outside of London. I worked there for four weeks before finding a job in the city in Marylebone, right near Regent's Park. I worked as the Pensions Manager for BNP Paribas, a French bank. I adhered to my vow of not losing myself in work, instead putting my head down and doing what needed to be done within normal hours, unless work required me to stay (such as during bonus time or for the issuing of stock options). I was fortunate to be in a building that enabled me to look out over the rooftops of London, meaning that I never suffered in the wintertime in the way that my boyfriend did – he worked in the financial district, going to work in the dark, coming home in the dark and looking out onto a brick wall all day long.

In our first three months of living in London we ate jam or peanut-butter sandwiches every day for lunch. We had to replenish our savings and get back on our feet. I was blissfully happy when we decided that we had saved enough, as it meant that I could buy something for lunch, even if it happened to be a New York pastrami sandwich from Pret-a-Porter. From that time on we rarely ate sandwiches, and on the weekends we would always head out or I would cook for us.

We had agreed that we wanted to save money for our return home, as the exchange rate was quite good at the time. Essentially, we did not want to return home broke. However, we wanted to also travel and see as much as we could, so we consciously chose not to partake in the normal Australian pastime of spending hours in the pub. Our weekends were spent as tourists in London, and due to our location we could walk to the Houses of Parliament, Big Ben and Westminster Abbey in half an hour. In fact, we walked a great deal around London and it set the tone for how I would choose to see any city that I travelled to. I feel that being on foot is the best way to connect with a city. You see things differently, as well as having the ability to find hidden treasures and places off the normal tourist trail.

One thing in which we did indulge was the arts – theatre, musicals, ballet and concerts. The Royal Albert Hall became a regular fixture, and a highlight for me was the Last Night of the

Proms. An Aussie girl turned into an emotional flag-waving British patriot, my voice raised to 'Rule Britannia', soaking up the emotion and the patriotism that I had never experienced before in Australia.

We went to see *The Nutcracker* at Christmas time, watched Ralph Fiennes in Shakespeare's *Richard III*, and saw the London productions of *The Phantom of the Opera*, *Les Miserables* and *Blood Brothers* (my favourite musical). We stood for way too long at the Globe Theatre in the traditional manner of Shakespeare's time, and felt disappointed when we watched *Cats*.

I loved lining up at 5.30am to score tickets to Wimbledon that same day – the strawberries and cream alone were worth the wait.

I also loved getting up early on a beautiful warm summer's day to line up along the fence down The Mall to watch the Trooping of the Colour. Our front row position was perfect as we watched the preparations, including the use of a ruler to measure the exact distance between each soldier along the route. I admired the stamina of the men who stood there in the heat, not moving, their bodies stiff, and their heads heavy with those black feathery hats. One close to us did not quite make it and fainted. We saw all of the royals up close and, by some stroke of luck (or grace of God), when they allowed the crowd to move towards Buckingham Palace at the end of the event, we ended up on the palace fence, the perfect vantage point for when the royals stepped out onto the balcony to watch the fly-past and wave at the crowd.

Living in London, I was in my element and I loved immersing myself in the traditions, pomp and ceremony. I loved being absorbed in history, knowing that I was walking in the footsteps of so many famous characters and personalities. I felt alive.

One of my favourite memories is of Christmas Eve 1999. We decided to attend midnight mass at Westminster Abbey. It was a cold and wet night but because public transport didn't run after midnight (or on Christmas Day), we had to go by foot. As we walked in the dark up the road that runs in front of the Houses of Parliament, we looked up and saw a wave of rain coming towards us. It was an awesome but eerie sight and we ran the last few hundred metres to the Abbey.

I was elated that we had decided to go. The Abbey is a place that I have always loved due to the history dripping from every corner, crevice and eave. But there was something even more extraordinary about sitting in a pew on Christmas Eve, the choir singing carols and hymns, the Abbey filled with sacred song, candles burning and ordinary people partaking in a festive tradition.

Winter was long and hard. I wore my winter coat for seven months, but in the springtime, as we walked through Hyde Park, the sight of bluebells, daffodils and snowdrops were enough to brighten my mood and keep me going. Watching nature spring back to life was one of my beloved pastimes, and walks through Hyde Park became a regular event. If you were there early in the morning, you might have been lucky enough to catch sight of the Queen's beautiful black horses being ridden through the park at a canter, their shiny coats glistening in the sunshine.

Being so close to Paris, I wanted to go there in each of the different seasons, if we could. In the autumn of 1999 we caught the Eurostar from Waterloo station, and three hours later we were in the City of Love and Light. From the moment my feet first touched the ground in France I felt at home and the feeling has never altered. I felt safe and relaxed and I was like a little girl in a candy store, the smile never leaving my face the entire weekend.

That first visit was all about the main sights. We journeyed to Paris again in winter (just prior to Christmas), and for a longer stay in the spring. Every season unveiled a new look for the Champs Élysées, my favourite season being winter, when the fairy lights, imitation snow and Christmas trimmings decorated the length of this most famous of boulevards. Each time we chose a different arrondissement in which to stay, allowing us to experience the different character and underlying energy that exists within them all. I took to the Metro as if I had lived there all of my life.

Paris is a city for walking and somehow I willed my legs to keep going, my insatiable appetite for exploring this beautiful city never truly satisfied – simply because there is so much to see and discover, to eat and experience. I would eat the most amazing *pain au chocolat* for breakfast – warm and crispy, the chocolate soft. We would buy fresh baguettes for lunch and fill them with brie, country terrine, or tomatoes and cheese, purchased from the local market. Dining in brasseries and bistros, sampling the classics such as beef bourguignon, French onion soup, steak and *frites* and crème brûlée and – yes, despite the way it is farmed – loving my first taste of foie gras.

As a treat, we once dined at night in a restaurant that overlooked the Arc de Triomphe – the food was almost trumped by the spectacular view. We experienced the Eiffel Tower in different ways: during the day ascending by elevator after having queued politely for some time; and at night taking the stairs to reach one of the most beautiful vistas I have ever laid eyes on. To stand at the top of the tower and gaze out upon a city that reaches into your soul is unforgettable.

The elegance of the Opéra quarter; the manicured gardens; hours spent wandering amongst exquisite works of art in the Louvre, Musée Rodin, Musée Picasso and Musée d'Orsay. A day trip out to the astonishingly beautiful Versailles; sitting at a typical Parisian café and people-watching – the stylish women walking by confident and feminine; shopping for sunglasses on the Champs Élysées and for clothes at Le Bon Marché (Paris' oldest and most stylish department store in the 7th arrondissement); and the charm of the cobblestoned streets in Montmartre – these were some of the many things we experienced during those visits.

There is so much to love about Paris. It truly was the beginning of a love affair that has never ceased and it is my dream to spend time living there one day.

The trip to Paris in the spring came at the end of four days in Amsterdam. My father was born in the Netherlands and, having arrived in Australia in 1950 at the age of two, he had never returned. I wanted to go on his behalf and see some of the country where his origins lay. Spring was the perfect time, of course, as the country was awash with fields of tulips in an array of colours. The Keukenhof gardens were simply spectacular, and it's worth planning a trip to the Netherlands just to see them. Due to our limited time, we chose to go on a couple of day tours to see as much as we could. I loved what I saw, especially Anne Frank's house and the Keukenhof gardens, but I did not feel a deep connection to the land. I knew that it was unlikely I would return but I felt I had paid my respects to a country whose energy ran through my veins regardless.

After 14 months of working in London, we decided (due to my boyfriend's homesickness, brought on by a long winter) that it was time to give up our flat and head off on a backpacking journey around Europe before heading home to Australia. We hired a car and spent 10 days driving around Britain and

Scotland, staying in B&Bs – although after day three I could not stand to wake up and eat another English cooked breakfast. We said goodbye to London in the August of 2000, flying out to Berlin, the first stop on a four-month journey travelling by train and bus through seven countries.

As I stepped onto that easyJet aircraft in London, bound for Berlin, I had no idea of the profound impact that the next four months would have on me. Until the end of this trip, I had no way of knowing how this travel experience would change my life or how much it would teach me.

In Berlin, a two-hour walking tour provided a history of World War II that no amount of schooling could possibly give you. Being there in person, seeing the bullet holes in the buildings, standing at Checkpoint Charlie and beside the Berlin Wall, walking in the Jewish Ghetto and watching as the city was starting to rebuild (in areas where buildings built by the Nazis had been demolished) was simply fascinating and I could not get enough.

Poland was about the Auschwitz-Birkenau concentration camp, which, for some reason, I was drawn to visit. Our visit was a profoundly emotional and thought-provoking day. We spent most of it in silence, our voices extinguished by the energy of a place where so many innocent people arrived and never left. Where unspeakable acts against humanity had taken place. Even that night, back in our room, we remained in silence, trying in our own way to process the images and words burnt into our eyes, the cries of the souls asking us to never, ever forget. I believe that unless you visit one of these places it is very hard to appreciate the size and horror of the Holocaust.

We caught an overnight train to Prague, where we were blessed with beautiful weather in a beautiful city, before moving on to Vienna and Salzburg. A long train journey to Italy followed, made stunning by autumn scenery through the Alps. Italy vies with France for a place in my heart.

Venice was simply magnificent, Milan a smart and fashionable city, Bologna chic and Verona romantic. The highlight of our time in Italy, though, was a week in a Tuscan villa with friends from Sydney. They had booked a place for three weeks and invited others to join them. We were lucky enough to time it with our visit and the adventure began when we were picked up in Siena. Waking up in the morning, stepping onto the cool terracotta Tuscan tiles and opening the shutters to reveal fields of grapevines was enough to make my soul sing. Added to that was touring of the hilltop villages, a day trip to the Italian Riviera, eating my most loved cuisine and sharing all of it with close friends – the whole experience left a permanent imprint on me.

I tasted truffle for the first time as part of a mouth-watering three-course meal at a restaurant set in the midst of the Tuscan hills. As we drove out of Florence after a day at the Uffizi gallery, I kept my head down in a book as we navigated the peak-hour traffic. How we came through that craziness without a scrape – when hundreds of cars seemed to converge, when no lanes were visible – was a miracle, and testament to my friend's nerve and driving skill.

The only downside was the rain, which had begun to fall two days in and would continue for weeks to come, following us as we moved onto France. From Florence, we caught the train to Nice, taking us along the Italian coastline and providing us with spectacular vistas and glimpses of the Mediterranean. We had one sunny day in Nice before torrential rain made it difficult to be a tourist but it did not stop us. We spent the next three weeks making our way around France, up to Lyon, Dijon, Beaune and the Champagne region before heading to Normandy.

Another history lesson was delivered as we toured the D-Day beaches. I was once again overcome by the enormity of what happened in World War II, especially when visiting the cemetery at Omaha beach and walking amongst the thousands of white crosses, the silence emanating emotion that only a hardened heart could not feel. Standing on Omaha beach, which was featured in the opening scenes of the movie *Saving Private Ryan*, it was abundantly clear that the men never stood a chance, a senseless tragedy of epic proportions.

After the intensity of our visit to Normandy, we relaxed on a train journey south to French Basque country, visiting the glamorous coastal town of Biarritz and the quaint and colourful fishing village of Saint Jean de Luz before entering Spain for five glorious weeks.

Tapas in the old town of Sans Sebastián: sherry poured theatrically into glasses; bar tops covered with the flavours and tastes of Spain (chorizo, paprika, jamon (ham), olives, prawns and more). The bar man keeping tabs on how much everyone had eaten; the floor littered with discarded napkins; the locals passing through for a snack on their way home from work. We savoured contemporary art at the Bilbao; the magic of Gaudí in Barcelona; an insight into the bizarre mind of Salvador Dalí; the exquisite beauty of the Alhambra in Grenada; a long lunch of paella at a restaurant facing the Mediterranean in Valencia; the Plaza de España (Square of Spain) in Seville; the cathedral-within-a-mosque in Cordoba; the walled old city of Toledo; and finally Madrid, a city with amazing museums and scrumptious food, including a simple plate of the delectable Iberico jamon enjoyed with a glass of sherry.

At night, we sat in a small softly lit room and felt the passion and spirit of flamenco; we stood alongside thousands of locals as the Christmas lights were turned on in the centre of the city; and we watched the majesty of the world game as Real Madrid played against a Belgian team. Spain was a country of contrasts between the Moorish south, the passionate Basque in the north and the patriotic Catalans around Barcelona.

It was time to head home – four months of a backpacker daily breakfast consisting of bananas and yoghurt most days had worn thin. (This was a cheap and readily available meal when staying in low-cost hotels that didn't offer breakfast. Because we were heading into winter while touring Spain, we were able to buy our breakfast the night before and hang it out the window overnight – the freezing night temperatures made for a natural fridge.)

We flew out of Madrid to London, and then out of Heathrow Airport on 10 December 2000 on a Qantas flight. We were thrilled to have been upgraded to business class following a two-hour wait after the computer systems crashed – it was there that I sipped Champagne in honour of a journey that had opened my heart, expanded my mind with history (both fascinating and tragically sad), and given me an appreciation for architecture and the results of creative passions. A journey that saw me fall in love with a continent where my heart felt at home and my tastebuds came alive, and where I had learned more about myself and the world than a classroom or a book had ever taught me.

A journey that showed me what it means to really live life – to work to live, not live to work. I love how the Europeans, especially in Italy, France and Spain, place importance on eating well and together, not rushing but sitting down, how families gather as one on Sundays and life is truly enjoyed. Travelling changed me in a good way and I have never regretted taking time out of my career or spending that amount of money to experience all that I did. I would not trade it for a thing and it was a reward for the long, long hours spent enclosed in an office and chained to a desk.

My travels put into perspective, for me, how lucky we are in Australia, a country that shares no border with another, allowing us to live without military conflict knocking on our doorstep every day. Despite my love of Europe, as the plane flew over Australia and the sun rose in the east, my heart skipped a beat. I was now home, ready to stop and settle in one place, and to catch up with loved ones.

It would be 12 months before I could face eating another banana. It would also be just over three years until I married my boyfriend, four years until I brought my first beautiful son into the world and only a matter of time before my world would start to come crashing down around me.

For You to Ponder

- If you haven't travelled out of your home country, is that something you would like to do? If so, how can you make it happen? Perhaps you could create a vision board?

- If you have travelled outside of your country, what did you learn about yourself and the world? Has travelling had a profound impact on you? If so, can you reflect on why?

Chapter 7
Motherhood Challenges Me

'Rest easy, real mothers. The very fact that you worry about being a good mom means that you already are one.'

~ Jodi Picoult

Motherhood has pushed me into the deepest recesses of my pain, opening up festering wounds, forcing me to look at myself in the mirror. To look at all of me, especially the parts that scared me and which I had rejected. It has brought up feelings of shame, guilt, remorse and failure. It has ultimately been the event that sent me hurtling towards my healing journey.

In many ways, this chapter has been the hardest to write. It was one of the last chapters that I wrote for this book. I have grappled with being authentic and speaking my truth – something that I am committed to – yet balancing that with writing in such a way that my love for my precious boys shines through.

Along with never aspiring to have a grand white wedding, I also never grew up with a longing to be a mother. It was not a burning fire in me that drove me in my decisions and choices as a young woman but it was something I knew I would experience. Saying that, as I approached 33 years of age, it did factor into some of my decisions, and at 34 I had my first child, James, as the sun set on the horizon.

My labour was long and I was exhausted. I did not sleep the first night after James was born, and sleep deprivation would terrorise me for the next six years, at times pushing me to the edge of my sanity. I loved my baby but I have to confess that I did not experience that overwhelming sense of love that some mothers talk about upon first meeting their newborn. I feel guilty even writing that, as if there is something so terribly wrong with me. I feel as though I allowed my early, negative experiences of motherhood to sow seeds of failure within my very being, and that feeling of failing as a mother is something I struggle with even now, 10 years later.

If I could go back, with the knowledge and wisdom that I have now, I would change many things. My nature is one of 'doing the right thing', and I know that many times I allowed the voice of my mother to drive my approach to motherhood, instead of choosing to connect to my own heart and intuition. Back then I certainly did not go with the flow as I do now, and I can see that I was fighting against nature, a battle that inflicted so much unnecessary wounding on both myself and, I am sure, my beautiful boy.

I was content with one child at that time but, out of a sense of wanting another child so that James had a sibling, we chose to try for a second. In reality, with the passing of time, I can see that I was suffering from postnatal depression and when I fell pregnant the second time, at the age of 35, I was very concerned that I would not cope with a second child.

When I suffered my miscarriage in early October 2006, there was probably an element of relief within me, and a sense that I had bought myself some time to try to 'fix' how I was feeling. A few weeks later I would take that first step in really healing myself. When I mentioned to a friend recently that I was struggling with starting this chapter she asked if I had healed my feelings around the miscarriage. Of course, my reply was, 'yes, I think I have'. But it did sit there at the back of my mind, a little niggle suggesting that perhaps I had not fully faced that loss.

So, two days ago, while being guided through a meditation where we were walking back in time, the knock-out punch came. The tears began to flow as the word 'miscarriage' rose up as an event where loss had occurred in my life. What I got so clearly is that I have been feeling guilty that the baby lost its life because I was not ready for it. At a deep, almost imperceptible level, I've been feeling that the miscarriage was my fault, that my body rejected life and that I should have known better and done better. I realised that those beliefs were fertiliser for that previously planted seed of motherhood failure, and that I have carried those unconscious beliefs within me every day since the miscarriage.

A year later I would give birth to my beautiful second baby, Liam, having to be induced as a matter of urgency due to a liver condition that I was suffering. If I'd thought that sleep deprivation was bad before, I would now discover the reasons why it is used as a means of torture. I honestly do not know how I got through some days. However, seeing James play with Liam, and the joy they found in each other, I knew I had made the right decision. Liam has a big heart, gives the best cuddles – which we call 'monkey cuddles' because of how he clings on with his arms and legs – and he has a cheeky twinkle in his brown eyes, which radiate joy as he practises his dance moves. I'm so glad that I didn't stop at one child.

There have been moments when the responsibility of being a mother has overwhelmed me and threatened to crush me. I do not take it lightly that I am a mother, and I am acutely aware, maybe too much so, that motherhood is not about making me feel better, complete or needed as a woman. It is about the sacred duty I have been gifted with, that of guiding two souls into becoming loving, responsible human beings who can make a positive impact on the world while giving their own truth and soul song an authentic voice.

I can see how I punish myself constantly when I do not live up to my high expectations of myself as a mother, when I do not handle something as well as I could have, when my 'stuff' blocks me from being the mother whom I know is in there somewhere. I have had many mummy moments that are less than perfect and over which I have crucified myself.

I know what it feels like to be at the mercy of a mother who is in pain, and I hate myself (yes, hate myself) when I allow that pain within me to paint a scar on my boys and the fabric of who they are. It is ultimately what drives me forward into the darkness, especially when I feel as if I cannot bear to come face to face with my pain one more time. I do not find it easy to accept that I am human and doing the best I can under the circumstances. I am my very own judge, jury and executioner.

If I feel I could have done better I will always, always apologise to my boys and tell them there is nothing they did to deserve how I reacted or handled the situation. I do not see my apology as a 'get out of jail free' card. I see it as showing them that I'm human, that I know I could have done better and that I will keep trying to become the best mum I can be – for they deserve no less and they are worth every bit of my own discomfort. When I know better, I do better. They are my greatest teachers, and are mirrors for what I need to heal.

Although I had wed with the full intention of staying married, my husband and I separated when my boys were 3½ years and one year of age. There were so many lessons to be learned from our separation, and I will share those learnings with you soon.

I find it difficult to rest in my softness and nurturing when I am trying to be both parents, working and running a household. I would not change the decision about ending my marriage but I sometimes wish I could relax more often and let that softness shine through, for it is where I feel happiest as a mum.

Despite the struggle that I have, at times, with motherhood, there are so many treasured memories and moments. I love watching their faces as they experience the world and something new. I love showing them the world and exposing them to all it has to offer. I love nurturing them when they are sick. I love starting my day with morning cuddles in my bed and I miss it if they do not come in. I shower them with kisses and cuddles and every day let them know that I love them. I love celebrating every one of their achievements and seeing them blossom into unique human beings. I love watching them play on the beach together for hours or hearing their laughter in those moments when sibling combat has been laid to rest. I love cooking with them in the kitchen and sitting at the Melbourne Cricket Ground, cheering on our favourite football team together. I could go on and on.

I am so very proud of their resilience and am acutely aware of all that they have gone through in their short lives already. I feel privileged and very proud to be their mum and honoured that they are such an integral part of my journey.

The three of us are very strongly connected and I know that they are here to help me fulfil my purpose in life. I never take their love lightly. I hope that one day I can look back and give myself a moment of acknowledgement that I did the best I could in every moment; that despite my sometimes less-than-perfect mothering, I always came from a place of love, where their wellbeing on every level was always my number one priority; that I took responsibility for my pain and owned it. Those are all things of which I know I can be proud. I hope that one day I can forgive myself for those moments of imperfection.

For You to Ponder

- If you are a mother, do you have moments where you really struggle in your role?

- Do you place high expectations on yourself?

- Can you see all the wonderful things that you achieve as a mother? I encourage you to write down three of your greatest achievements so far, as a mother. Just waking up and getting out of bed every day is sometimes an achievement!

- If you are a single mother, do you reach out for help and ensure that you take care of yourself?

Chapter 8
Help Me, Please!

'Understanding is the first step to acceptance, and only with acceptance can there be recovery.'

~ JK Rowling

'I cannot do this. I am going mad. I am dying inside. I feel suffocated and tortured by pain, screaming silently, "please, please help me, I do not want to feel like this for one second longer". I want to run away, to a place where no one can find me, where I can curl up in a ball and not be responsible for anyone or anything. I do not want to talk and I feel as though I have nothing left to give.'

This was the moment in time, on a sunny day in November 2006 (two years prior to my marriage crumbling), when I finally reached a point where I knew I could not live one more day feeling the way that I did. An internal tsunami was drowning me and I was so very close to being totally consumed by it. I needed help.

I searched frantically for the business card of a psychologist who had been recommended to me by my GP months before – not because I had asked for it or expressed that I was struggling but because she must have sensed that I was not okay. She could see clearly what I could not admit out loud. I looked everywhere but could not find that card and yet I knew that I had kept it.

On my knees and crying, my auntie's name came into my head. She was like a mother to me and was someone in whom I could confide and trust, a feeling I did not have with my own mother. I picked up the phone and called her, grateful beyond measure that she was at home and had answered the phone. My heart bled into the phone, my eyes wept rivers of pain and my auntie quietly listened, expressing gentle words of love and understanding. She told me that she could see my grandmother and my brother with me in that moment, that they were behind me, providing strength and love. This made me weep more as I had always wished that my big brother were still with us, somehow sensing that he would be there for me when I really needed him. Following a thought that had come into her head, she gave me the name of someone to call.

I made the call immediately, booked an appointment and my healing journey began. Funnily enough, I found the business card for the psychologist the next day in a very obvious spot where I had, of course, looked. The grace of God had been at work, guiding me to the right person, and since that moment I have always trusted that grace will, in fact, lead me home.

Throughout this entire episode, while I was sobbing and talking to my auntie, James – who was 18 months old – played happily outside, coming in every now and then, seeing me, smiling, almost saying to me, 'yay! She is finally getting the help she needs. Go mum!'. It would be the first of many moments when I could see in his face, his eyes and his body language, and hear in his voice, that his soul was speaking to me, telling me that I was on the right track. Those moments have been very profound, and in recalling them now I feel in my heart the energy from his soul.

The reality was that I had been struggling internally since 1998. I had visited a psychologist in Sydney before travelling overseas and on my return to Melbourne in 2003, when I was on the brink of suffering a nervous breakdown. Of course, both times I felt better afterwards, having voiced some of my issues, which were like parasites eating away at me. In truth, the sense of relief that I gained lasted a relatively short time, for it never touched the real source of my pain. The event that nudged me towards this life-changing crisis point was the miscarriage I had had a few weeks prior.

When I had fallen pregnant the second time I felt nervous. I did not feel good within myself, I sensed all was not okay within my marriage and I secretly worried about how I would cope with another baby. We had arrived in Sydney for a couple of weeks to attend a wedding. However, the day after we arrived, James, who was only 17 months old, became ill. Within 24 hours he was so sick that we rushed him to hospital.

As we were walking out the door on the way to the hospital, I had a sudden urge to go to the toilet. When I went, there was blood; not a good sign when you are pregnant. We arrived at the emergency department and had James seen to. I then quietly mentioned what I had found. After James was settled into his room and placed on a drip for fluids and IV antibiotics, I went by myself for an ultrasound. I received the news that the baby had died and as a result I would need a procedure. In that moment I felt very alone. I returned to James' room and began to cry as I told my husband. James suddenly woke up. I stopped myself from crying and put on a brave face. James needed me and I had to be strong.

Late the following night, as my little boy lay in his hospital crib with his father by his side, I lay on a stretcher, preparing to go into surgery to have the little life cleaned out of me. The life I had been so worried about bringing into the world due to my mental state. I was wheeled up the corridor towards the lift, and, just as the lift doors began to close, my mother-in-law ran in to wish me luck, tears in her eyes, many words not needing to be spoken. Her gesture would leave an imprint on my soul. I woke up a short while later, was given sleeping pills for the next two nights, and my mother-in-law drove me home. The pills helped me to ignore the feelings I had already squashed earlier that day. I felt nothing. I did not cry.

My son would remain in hospital for 3½ days. I never made it to the wedding. I felt grateful that all of this had occurred in Sydney, where I felt loved and supported by my husband's family, something I knew I would not have received from my own family. However, a few weeks later it was clear that ignoring how I felt about the miscarriage had simply pushed me to breaking point. I am sure, without a doubt, that I would not have coped with a new baby at that time and the miscarriage was nature's way of agreeing with me.

When the therapist opened the door, on 6 December 2006 (serendipitously, this was my aunt's birthday), I knew in an instant that I was exactly where I was meant to be. I felt as if I had come home. She is a transformational therapist, working with you to dig deep and find the origin of the weeds that represent all the pain and issues that you carry. This is what I wanted. I wanted a cure, not just a temporary solution that I had experienced in the past. I wanted to transform my life into something that had meaning and which was a true reflection of who I am. Driving home after that first session, my life flashed before me and I could see why I had made many of my decisions.

For the next five years, she would listen, hold my heart in her hands, guide me, share her wisdom and her gifts, help put me back together, help me break through the illusions. It was the beginning of my spiritual awakening. Importantly, she validated my feelings and was the first person to gently suggest that I was not responsible for others or their actions. I would learn that just having someone hold the space, listen and be a witness to your story was deeply healing in itself. I began to see the 'greater' meaning of life that I had for so long sensed and yearned for.

My therapist pointed out that I was effectively wounding myself every time I denied my truth and entered the family space when I really did not want to – the feeling was akin to inflicting deep cuts upon my body, my heart and my soul. Having moved back to Melbourne in 2003, my descent into darkness had only increased. Feelings of guilt around what I 'should' do were like a corrosive liquid that ate away at my insides. I had been completely ignoring my own truth and myself. I came to recognise that the close relationship I believed I had with my mother was not really so.

I faced the realities of my choices and my relationships. I took a good hard look at myself and accepted the part I had played in relationships and situations. On some level I had allowed myself to be treated a certain way. I had expended so much energy trying to make others happy, yet one day I woke up to see that nothing I did was making a difference, and that making others happy was not my job – my own happiness was all I was responsible for. I could see a pattern within myself of doing it in order to be accepted and loved.

There is a dance between two people in any relationship, and the story and pain that each brings into every encounter determines the choreography. It does not serve you in the long run to place all of the blame on another, especially when, as an adult, you are in control of your choices and your reactions. There is something immensely freeing about owning your part and taking responsibility. It makes you human, builds compassion for others and allows you to see that there is no such thing as perfection. That we are all here trying to do the best we can with what we know at the time.

Starting this journey forced me to get in touch with what it was I really wanted – what I wanted for my relationships, what I wanted for my life, how I wanted to feel, and to be clear about what held great meaning for me. I would escape to the country for a day, clear my head and be still, allowing my heart to whisper to me, to share what it yearned for me to know. I listened, I wrote in my journal and I allowed myself to breathe into it. As I sat with nature, I allowed myself to begin to dream that things really could be different. Hope sprouted, and as I slowly began to claw back the power that I had given away, my determination to see it through to the end grew.

Those insights and notes about what I truly wanted for my life, and the direction I wanted to go, became the foundation for all of my decisions. They became the lighthouse that guided me when the inevitable darkness and storms formed, when doubt and fear threatened to smash me on the rocks. All I can say is: thank goodness for the sturdiness of that lighthouse, for I had no idea about the intensity of the storm that was brewing.

For You to Ponder

- Do you give yourself permission to cry, to feel your feelings and your pain? If not, why not?

- Do you take time out to be still and quiet and to listen to what your heart yearns for you to hear? If not, why not?

- Can you recognise when the Universe has sent the perfect person to help you in your time of need?

Chapter 9
I Did It Before Gwyneth

*'Stepping onto a brand new path is difficult,
but not more difficult than remaining in a situation,
which is not nurturing to the whole woman.'*

~ Maya Angelou

When I began my healing journey in 2006, my marriage was starting to hit shaky ground. My journal from that time reflects concerns that we were drifting apart and that I was unsure what the future held for us. All I knew was that I needed to work on myself and heal what was wounded and broken within me.

As part of my healing I wrote down what I wanted in a partner and a relationship, something I confess to never having done before. My deepest desire was that my marriage would survive and we would find a path to walk down that honoured both of our needs. But, looking back, I think I knew what the outcome was going to be and it unsettled me.

In 2008, we hit a fork in the road; issues that had been present from early on became insurmountable obstacles, and for our own reasons we each chose to take a different path into the future. For my part, if we could not join each other on the same path, I wanted to end the marriage before we hated each other, before we had inflicted untold emotional damage on our children and before there was little chance that we could ever co-parent in a healthy way together.

I was nearing 40 and I knew that I wanted to be loved and give love. I did not want to allow 10 years to go by and watch myself slowly die inside. I wanted my boys to have a different example of how a marriage should be. Ultimately, I wanted my boys to have a happy mum and a happy dad. Yes, I have always wanted my ex to find love and be happy, for he deserves that as much as I do. If I could not meet his needs then I wanted to set him free to find someone who could.

Financial considerations and the challenges of single motherhood never factored into my decision-making. Their importance was insignificant to me, compared to my emotional wellbeing and that of my boys. I placed my trust in God and myself that all would be okay. It was a simple case of the vision being greater than the fear.

From the moment we decided to consciously uncouple – yes, Gwyneth, we did it way back in 2008 and I am sure many others had before us – I was adamant that my boys would not be in a position of having to choose between us. We had decided to have children together and we needed to step up to that responsibility and not have them become the carnage of our choices. It has not always been easy, but we have spent every one of the boys' birthdays, and every Christmas, together. The boys have never had to split their time between the two of us on occasions like that. We managed to do some day trips together when the boys were younger, and we work together as well as we can to ensure they come first. If I need my ex because one of the boys is very ill and needs to go to hospital, he is always there, taking time off work to look after the other one. He does not play games with drop-off times and he honours his financial commitments. He continues to be a part of their lives and our post-divorce relationship is always a work in progress.

The truth is, there were times in the first couple of years when it was very hard to stop myself from letting the anger consume me. When we were negotiating the financial settlement I had moments when I thought I would never speak to him again. But I kept the long-term goal in front of me, a signpost that stopped me from going off course when we hit those inevitable bumps in the road. It was not easy and it took a great deal of energy at times but I am glad that I made the choice that I did.

I am aware that the boys may have experienced wounding from their parents not being together. Of course, they wish at times that we were both in the same house but I simply tell them that we would not be happy, that their dad and I living together would make everyone unhappy. I tell them that, with their parents living separately, they get the best of both of us. What I do know is that outsiders noticed a positive change in both boys, particularly James, my eldest, when we made the decision to go our separate ways. Teachers have commented that they would never have guessed that my boys' parents were divorced and in those moments I feel proud of the decisions I have made.

Drawing on my own experiences as a child and a mother, I believe that children, no matter what the age, know that something is not okay between their parents. They sense it and when they are young they are without the emotional intelligence to know what is happening. They just know that something is out of balance. I sensed it and I know my boys knew it with us, too.

From my later studies in holistic counselling, I learned that when you badmouth, criticise or verbally attack your ex in front of your children, you are effectively saying to them (the children) that there is a part of them that you reject or do not like. For the truth is that a part of their father and mother resides within them – we all have a bit of both. So if you reject the father and call him a loser, you are, on a subtle level, saying to the child, 'you are also a loser'. When I learned this I was grateful that I had chosen not to attack him, even when I did not like what he was doing. This wisdom has stayed with me as a reminder to never go down this road in the future. It is also true that I had loved my ex enough to decide to have children with him, so why would I wish him ill and cast him out onto the trash heap now?

I was blessed to have the support of my in-laws and his family. They were shocked by the decision but did not take sides. They also put the welfare of the boys at the top of their list, and the boys maintain a close and healthy relationship with them all. I know they consider me to still be a part of the family and I also know that if I ever really need them they will be there. I am acutely aware that this is a rarity and I give them full points for rising above everything.

After my divorce, I made a conscious decision to remain single and to work on healing myself. It took five years before I entered another relationship, and even then it showed that I had more work to do on healing wounds from my marriage and childhood. I was very clear that I did not want to enter into relationship after relationship, repeating the same patterns and rocking my boys' foundations at the same time. That is not to say that I have not longed for a man in my life or despaired of ever finding love again, as I have felt both. However, stability for my boys has always been paramount.

I felt that, as my boys were young, my responsibility lay in navigating them through the changes and making sure I could limit as much as possible any long-lasting effects. This is one area where I do acknowledge that I have done a good job and I am proud of myself for holding love in my heart every step of the way.

On my wedding day in 2004 I believed that my marriage would last forever. Or did I? Consciously, I certainly did, and as I said my vows that evening I meant them. However, looking back, I can see the signs that I missed, or refused to really listen to. A couple of times, there was an inner knowing that this marriage was not going to last, but this was balanced by a similar knowing that, despite everything, within the deepest part of my being I knew we were meant to be together for the time that we were. He was the person who pushed me to release a primal knowing that 'I am worth it'. For that I have nothing but gratitude.

I have never regretted our time together. I know without a doubt that I would go through the same process again in order to come out the other side with the growth, clarity and insights that I received. I now know that there is nothing worse than feeling lonely in a relationship, and that we are all worthy of more, of living our truth and of receiving the love we deserve. I know I can hold my head high, look my boys in the eye and tell them that I did everything I could within my power to fix what was wrong. Ultimately I am only responsible for me and I hope they see that I had the courage to speak my truth with an acute awareness of the impact on them.

For You to Ponder

- Are you still connected to yourself as a woman if you are now a wife/partner and mother?

- Are you clear within yourself about what you want from a relationship, and about what qualities you want in a partner?

- If you have come through a relationship breakdown, have you healed the pain from that experience so that you don't take it into the next relationship and project past hurts onto your new partner?

- Have you taken time to nurture and care for yourself after a relationship breakdown?

- Have you taken responsibility for the part you played in the breakdown of a relationship? (Remember, it is never 100% one way – we are all co-creators.)

Chapter 10
Betrayal Breaks Me

'You may shoot me with your words,
you may cut me with your eyes,
you may kill me with your hatefulness,
but still, like air, I'll rise!'

~ Maya Angelou

My marriage breakdown was one life event that helped to shape who I am. However, my major growth experience has been through relations with my family of origin and how those relations suddenly turned sour.

I had started to step outside the box, to listen to my needs, to not do things because I felt I 'should', to visit when I had pure intention and longing in my heart, to honour my truth. I realised that I did not resonate with my family and had begun to put distance between them and myself. Little was I to know that by choosing love over fear it would unleash a darkness that almost extinguished the light I was walking towards.

For a year I recall sensing an undercurrent of 'something' going on in my family. I had no evidence or clear idea of why I felt this but it was a time when my intuition and inner knowing knew that something was not right. Have you ever felt that internal unrest or niggle that will not go away?

My intuition knew something that I was not ready to see or hear consciously. I chose not to tell my family about the decision my husband and I had made to separate, because I wanted to get through Christmas. I think I sensed that the reaction and support I hoped for would not eventuate, and with two young children it was easier to keep the façade going during an already stressful time.

That Christmas, in 2008, was the first time my mum relinquished her role as the host, and allowed one of my sisters to host it. I thought my sister had done really well to convince her to do this. Unfortunately, I would discover a few weeks later that the reason was much more sinister, and to do with me. This would be the last Christmas I would spend with my family.

On New Year's Eve, the boys and I stayed with my parents. I chose to tell my parents that night about our separation. I do not know what I was expecting but the reaction I received was cold and distant. No questions or concern about how I was feeling, how the boys were, what was I going to do, and definitely no hugs or display of warmth and love. I felt alone, and in that moment I had a further sense that all was not okay. I knew innately that I was on my own, that my parents would not be my safe place to fall as I navigated the emotions of divorce.

That night, after everyone was in bed, I had the strangest conversation with my mum. We talked in a way we had never done before (not in a good way; rather, different and unsettling) – she looked me in the eye and said she loved me unconditionally, no matter what happened. I looked straight back at her and said with clarity and strength, 'no, you do not'. She never argued, but walked away. I asked her to keep the news of my separation to herself as I wished to tell my sisters. The gnawing sense of an approaching storm gathered momentum within me.

The evening of 7 February 2009, the day of the Black Saturday bushfires, marked the beginning of the veil being lifted. I felt as though I was walking into a black hole, with no idea of the force that was propelling me into it.

The morning after Black Saturday, an urge rose up from deep within, telling me that I had to go to visit my father, who was in respite care in Castlemaine. I drove up playing a CD, singing the *Moola Mantra* (a Sanskrit mantra that invokes the presence of God) over and over – not knowing the words, but it somehow giving me comfort and allowing me to stay focused on the road. I would learn later that the last line of the mantra is, 'Om, the divine absolute truth'. I was about to receive the absolute truth in the days ahead.

It took 90 minutes to drive up the freeway from Melbourne to Castlemaine. The visit with my father lasted 15 minutes. I had let him know that I was coming and it was clear that something had gone on between the time of my call to him and my arrival. I asked some questions about the past but was essentially dismissed and I cried for the entire journey home. That visit would take me even closer to the precipice of that black hole where I would enter an internal darkness which, at the time, seemed endless and vast, and my relationship with my family would be shattered within 48 hours.

After the visit to Dad, I attended my yoga class on the Tuesday evening. For some reason, a bowl of Tiger's Eye crystals (a stone of protection) at the class caught my eye. I knew I needed to buy one. That night, my youngest sister rang me and confessed what had been going on behind my back for the previous 12 to 18 months. It took great courage for her to make that admission and apologise for the part she had played. I am forever grateful that her heart whispered to her the truth of who I am.

It seems that stepping out of the box, and not playing the same role that I had previously done, had resulted in untrue stories and unfounded accusations being spread about me. It seems that my healing journey had not been viewed very well.

I would discover that Christmas 2008 was about 'protecting' everyone from me, that dad's carers and others were being told of my 'evil' nature and that only the strongest were on duty when I was present so that they could 'withstand' me. I was accused of being after my parents' money, of being evil since birth, of being responsible for my oldest sister's behaviour throughout her life, and of going to the dark side. They also believed that James (who was three years of age) had joined me on the dark side, and that I was part of a cult that included my auntie and friends.

What disturbed me, to my very core, was that my mother was apparently doing 'something' to protect my Liam from me, and from him joining me on the dark side. The list goes on and includes many more lies and assertions about my marriage and things I had allegedly done.

When I got off the phone from the call with my sister, I could barely breathe and my body went into shock, shaking. With tears flowing down my face, I felt within me a surge of love for my two innocent boys and myself. In that moment, never was it so clear to me that enough was enough. I decided that my parents and my oldest sister would never see my boys or me again. I would not continue to put myself in a position where people could hurt me simply because I was being me, because I refused to play my old role in the family anymore, because I was choosing to live my life differently and because I had chosen to seek help and heal my own pain.

I would not continue to allow myself to be a victim of unhealed pain or because I saw beyond the façade of 'family togetherness' that had been erected. Most importantly, I vowed that my boys would never feel the way I had felt as a result of my family's choices. Involving my two innocent, beautiful young boys in this madness had crossed a line and the lioness within me rose up.

That night, clutching my Tiger's Eye crystal tightly in my hand, I curled up in the foetal position and wept tears of deep sorrow. The words played over and over in my mind. Is that who I am? What had I done to be treated this way? Have I lost my mind? Is this really happening? Is it really my own family that has done this, that has spread these horrible, horrible lies? I would lay awake until the early dawn, falling into an exhausted sleep for a short while.

For me, this was a betrayal that cut me down to my very core. I find it hard to express in words how I was feeling. The closest way of describing how I felt are the words that a girlfriend expressed to me after seeing my face the next day. At the time I could not tell her what had happened, but she would say later that I looked 'broken'. I felt broken in every way, and the next four weeks, maybe even longer, are a blur – I don't remember much from that time. I think I existed in body only, my spirit crushed, my heart broken. It felt as though the wrecking ball had fallen on any last hope that my family would sort out its issues, and on any hope that I could finally enjoy healthy and close relationships with my sisters, mum and dad.

I am so grateful to my sister-in-law, who was living with us at the time, as she helped to look after the boys. Despite being separated from each other, my husband was as much of a support as he could be. I do not know what I would have done without them both.

Two weeks after finding out about this betrayal, and having sat with my pain and reflected on what was the best thing for me to do, I would write to my parents and my oldest sister. I told them that I had learned of what they had been saying, and I advised them they were no longer welcome in my life. I wrote the letters with love in my heart, choosing for my anger to be expressed in other ways at another time. I finished by wishing them all well, by telling them I would always love them and by stating that I trusted that the truth would come out in the end – as Mum had always taught us, growing up.

I wanted to write the letters with a sense of empowerment, and with full understanding of the consequences of the choice I was making. At the time I felt that I had no other option, for I did not feel safe, in an emotional sense, being around them any longer. I wanted the letters to express my truth and reflect my choice to live from a place of love and light and not fear.

With a sense of peace but also an element of nervousness, I posted those letters. I knew the seriousness of the choice I had just made. Despite the fallout that would follow, it was my first step towards freedom. Freedom that would not be won without facing many dark days ahead – but I was on my way.

For You to Ponder

- Now that you are an adult, can you reflect on whether you are conscious in your relations with your family, even if your upbringing was happy?

- Are you playing a role within your family that is far from being your truth?

- Do you put on a mask and 'suffer' to stay in a family because you think you 'should'?

- Consider the following quote – does it resonate with you in any way? If so, why and where in your life are you doing this?

'You should not have to rip yourself into pieces to keep others whole.'

~ HpLyrikz.com

Chapter 11
Family Catastrophe

'Forgiveness is giving up the hope that the past could have been any different…'

~ Oprah Winfrey

The delivery of those letters was a catastrophic event that would shatter my family into fragments so tiny that trying to put the pieces back together has so far proven impossible. It was the final outcome in a story of how unhealed pain can infect following generations with a sickness that seems incurable.

The fallout reverberates to this day, and resembles a wasteland. Toxic residue was widespread and the contamination was so deep that years of healing would only scratch the surface. My youngest sister would become a target and would also end up cutting ties with my mother. My mum discarded my oldest sister once I had been informed about their beliefs that I had gone to the 'dark side'. Fingers were pointed and responsibility was avoided, denied even to this day. I know that many people continue to be provided with an inaccurate picture of events but I stand firm in myself, knowing that one day the truth will be told.

My brother looked at me as if I was a stranger when I turned up to tell him about the letters I was about to send. How could he understand when he had never been treated the way that my sisters and I had? It was our word against Mum's. In the end I simply lost contact with him, as I did not wish to place him in the impossible position of being in the middle.

I know that the fallout was not my responsibility but was a result of the choices that each person made. That is not to say that there have not been times when a sense of responsibility has crept in and I have wondered whether everyone would still be together if I had not made the choice that I did. I know that it is unlikely to be true. Everyone has their own reasons for the choices they made, and the way they reacted to their pain, and the consequences are their fate to carry and their story to tell.

I would go through my divorce alone, with no family around to support me or be there for me in my darkest days. It was a choice I had made consciously and, while there were many days when I wished it could have been different, I accepted that I could not change the reality of the past or the way people were.

I would spend the best part of the next four or five years unpacking the lessons contained in this experience, healing the wounds inflicted upon my soul and seeking some level of understanding for what drove this madness to occur. I faced the rawness of my pain. Questions around 'why?' were the most painful for me. My heart had always yearned for the kind of closeness that many women enjoy with their sisters and mother. My intentions always came from love, and I was generous and eager to help when I could.

I really struggled to understand why this had happened when I had always been the responsible one, the one they had turned to to help out in times of need, to pick up the reins and carry on for them. It took a lot of willpower to go within and find the truth that I had not done anything to deserve this, that I had been a good daughter and a good sister. To confirm that even though I was never perfect (who is?), I was not the person that I had been accused of being. I had to learn to hold that belief close to my heart. I had to ensure that any self-doubt did not become a cancer that slowly ate away at whatever self-belief remained.

Against all odds, I would find within myself love and compassion for all in my family. I have forgiven them all, in my own way, and continue to wish them well and send them love. With the help of many therapists and through the healing work I have done, I have been able to view from a higher perspective how the story, the entanglements, the grief, the generational patterns and every human's innate desire to be loved and accepted had been the fuel to ignite and keep this destructive fire going.

I could also see that this betrayal had, in fact, been a huge gift of learning for me and had helped me to grow and evolve in so many positive ways. I showed myself that I deserved better, that I loved myself enough to say 'no more'. I realised that I did not need to sacrifice myself for another person's love. I showed that I had a strong sense of self by holding onto the fact that I knew I was a good person and more. Therefore, it could be said that the situation was perfect and just what I needed in order for me to step onto the path of fulfilling my passion and purpose in this life.

As a result of my experience, I do not advocate the sentiment that 'blood is thicker than water'. Just because people are family does not give them the right to treat you in any way they like. It is not a free pass to ill treatment. There are times when the only course available is to leave an environment in which it's not healthy for you to be. Relationships can only be healed when both parties can come together with an open heart, a willingness to take responsibility for their behaviour and choices. Any relationship that means you need to sacrifice your truth, deny your voice or compromise your soul needs to be questioned.

I have always trusted that if we were meant to come back together and heal, Spirit would guide me through my inner knowing. Having said that, I have always had the sense that I would not see my mother again in this lifetime. With regards to my oldest sister and my dad there has always been a 'maybe' feeling.

Nearly 4½ years after sending the letters that brought about the fracturing in my family, I had a sudden, overwhelming urge to play my ABBA CDs daily. I was obsessed, singing, crying and replaying them over and over again. As the week wore on I began to feel a deep calling to go and visit my father, who I had been told was now in permanent care in Castlemaine. Spirit had called to me through music, choosing ABBA, as my love of that band was something I had inherited from my dad. I did not understand why this calling suddenly rose within me, but I went with it, not forcing it but waiting until the path I had to travel was clear.

So it was that on a Sunday morning in early October 2013, after I had tortured my boys with ABBA for a week, I woke up and sat outside in my quiet place and asked the question, 'Am I to go and visit my dad today?'. A clear and insistent response of, 'yes, yes, yes' came back, and, being an obedient person when it comes to the voice in my head (my intuition), I drove up to visit my dad. I hadn't seen him during all of those years; I felt terribly nervous and wasn't sure that I had the strength to go through with it.

It was a strange visit, and my dad acted as though nothing had happened or changed. I am sure it was a shock to have me turn up unannounced after so long. The conversation was polite. I was shocked at the deterioration in his health and I came away sensing that he may have lung cancer. Driving back to Melbourne, I once again felt as if I was in shock. I still had no understanding of why I had had the urge to visit and I just felt raw and vulnerable once again.

After that visit I 'sat' with the experience and allowed the reasons and wisdom to be unveiled in the right time. I would not visit him again until six months later, when the next urge arose. That visit would turn out to be a very different experience and I have continued to heal my relationship with him, having conversations that should have taken place many years ago. I feel incredibly blessed to have had this opportunity, especially as he is now terminally ill with lung cancer.

I have always had a feeling of deep inner peace about the decision to remove myself from my family. For me, it really was a matter of psychological and spiritual safety. I was watching the *Oprah* show one day, and I saw director, producer and actor Tyler Perry talk about his life and his relationship (or lack thereof) with his father, and he made a statement that would come to express perfectly why I made my decision. He said something along the lines of, 'as a child I had no choice or control over what happened to me, but as an adult I can choose to no longer be a victim'. Ultimately, I had made the decision to choose a different outcome for my life and that of my boys, an outcome that had love – not fear – as its essence.

Importantly, as a result of this experience, the friendships and relationships I now seek in my life are based on a foundation of truth and honesty. Lack of truth has been a deeply wounding issue throughout my life, meaning that I value strongly that I will receive an honest and truthful response to questions, that I can trust people's intentions and that my heart will not be taken for granted.

Family Catastrophe

I am not someone who needs to have a lot of people around me to make me feel good about myself, for I have learned that only I have the power to make me feel that way. It's important that the connections I make are authentic and heart-based – I am blessed that this is what I now receive. You, too, can choose to have that in your life, without needing to go through any pain to get it.

> *'Surround yourself with people who make you hungry for life, touch your heart and nourish your soul.'*
>
> *~ unknown*

For You to Ponder

- Can you reflect on painful situations in your life and see the gift or treasure contained in that experience?

- As you reflect, are you able to see how you grew as a person? How were you changed in a positive way as a result of that experience?

- Can you arrive at a place where you are able to thank the person involved in that painful situation for the gift of learning or growth that you received? You don't need to thank them in person; you can simply thank them in your journal.

Chapter 12
Circle of Gratitude

'We must find time to stop and thank the people who make a difference in our lives.'

~ John F Kennedy

In 2009, despite feeling as though I was in a pressure cooker, I decided that I wanted to honour myself and the progress I had made, as well as acknowledge and express gratitude for some of the women in my life who had touched my soul deeply. At this point in my journey it was important for me to tell these women – a group that included family, friends and healers – face to face why they meant so much to me.

The date was set for 22 November 2009 and I called it 'A Celebration and Gratitude for a Thousand Choices on My Journey Home to Self'. It was about healing, about honouring myself as a woman and as a mother and, in doing so, honouring all women and mothers. It was a day of celebration, gratitude and new beginnings.

I chose the term 'a thousand choices' after it was pointed out in a conversation that it had not just been the big decisions that had got me to where I was. It had been the thousand little choices that I made (that we all make) each and every day, in every moment.

For me, it was more than just gathering the women in a circle. It was the energy and preparation, the love and care that I put into preparing the space and the celebration. I shopped for brunch at my favourite food stores. I bought gorgeous sunflowers and vibrant red kangaroo paw from my favourite florist. I created a space that reflected me and my love and gratitude for the women who would be present. The oil that I chose to burn, the way that I set up the room, the way that I laid the table with food, all of it was done mindfully and with great love.

After enjoying brunch, I gathered the women in my lounge room and began my ceremony. I explained to the women gathered that I had invited them because they had, in some way, made an imprint on my soul or played an important role in my journey and healing. I expressed that I wanted to show my gratitude and honour them in front of the other women in the room.

Speaking to each woman from my heart, I told her the reason why she had imprinted my soul. There were tears and there were hugs. I presented each woman with a Red Coral crystal, as a token of my gratitude. I was drawn to the Red Coral crystal due to it being known as a 'woman's stone'. It also helps one to come into harmony with the natural forces of the Universe and with the wilderness within one's own being – along with quieting the emotions and bringing peace within the self.

I shared the following poem, which accompanied a painting that I'd created, and I invited the women to raise a glass of Champagne in honour of us all.

'Joy'

My joy has arisen from my pain,
Despite my sorrow, I had much to gain.

Love, truth and freedom called me from afar,
I was in a place where many are.

Suffocating, hurting, weeping inside,
Now I can look at myself with pride.

For I have fought to lift myself high,
From a darkness that was blacker than the night sky.

Sunshine, hope, light and love now reign,
That darkness will never hold me again.

For I have found my truth, my light, my SELF,
My true nature is taking its place on the shelf.

Today is the day that I, Jody, am born,
My soul is awake and singing, no longer forlorn.

So raise your glass, let your heart smile,
For a journey, a birth, that has taken a while.

An expression of the joy I felt about my life in 2010

As I sat reflecting after everyone had left, I felt a deep sense of peace, a knowing that I had arrived at a place where I could express my gratitude and show these women that small, everyday, seemingly ordinary acts can have a profound impact on a person. The feedback I received as the women left was that it had also been a powerful experience for them, and a couple of the women indicated their desire to hold one of their own ceremonies as they approached significant birthdays.

Nearly five years later, on 30 May 2014, I would come to feel an even deeper sense of appreciation and peace for having held this gratitude ceremony. My dear, beloved auntie, who had attended the ceremony on that day in 2009 and about whom I had felt the most emotional when giving my thanks, was killed instantly. No time for goodbyes, no time to tell her that I loved her. I took comfort that I had honoured her, and that I'd told her, to her face and in front of other women, the impact she had had on me, and why. I felt blessed that I had not left unsaid words of love and gratitude.

Reading the poem that had I penned back then, I realise how naïve I was to think that I was through the darkness. On reflection, I had really only begun to birth myself and I have travelled far in that birthing process since then, reaching into the depths – albeit with a greater strength and more solid foundation. In reality, I feel that it's only now that my birth is nearing completion, but I love that my innocence back then saw my life and myself in this way.

For You to Ponder

- When we are finding our way out of challenging times and darkness it may seem as though there is little to be grateful for. However, I have found that there are always so many blessings in our lives – when we sit quietly and reflect with an open heart and mind, we will find them. Consider using your journal to list items of gratitude.

- To honour the women who have made a positive impact on your life, I encourage you to hold your own Circle of Gratitude – for suggestions to get you started, see the 'Circle of Gratitude: Creating Your Own Ceremony' chapter later in this book.

Chapter 13

A Letter to My Boys

'The love of a mother is the veil of a softer light between the Heart and the Heavenly Father.'

~ Samuel Taylor Coleridge

Writing a letter to my two precious boys – in an attempt to explain why I had made certain decisions in my life – was something I wanted to do. I hoped that, if I did, when they were old enough and began asking more questions in search of a deeper understanding, I had something to give them. As always, I trusted that I would know when the time was right, and so on 11 April 2010 I awoke and knew that this was the day I would write my letter.

I share this deeply personal letter with you in the hope that it resonates with even one person about the impact that our pain, when ignored and unhealed, can have on our children.

To my dearest James and Liam,

I wanted to write this letter, so that one day, if you needed to, you could read this and maybe come to understand why I made some of the choices I have made.

Finding Freedom... Finding Me

I began a journey to reclaim my true self on 6 December 2006. At that time I was on my knees, overcome with pain, hurt, confusion, betrayal, lies and grief. At times I almost couldn't get out of bed and on some mornings I just wanted to run away. On that day, though, I began my journey out of those depths in the hope that I would reach the light, and that when I got there I would find my true self and an inner peace that I craved.

Also driving me on was you, James. A happy, beautiful little boy who brought so much joy to our lives, who enriched the lives of others and whom I wanted to protect. I also did not want to bring another child into our family (you, Liam) until some things had been resolved and I was in a better place.

For me, I did not and do not want either of you to ever experience the lack of love, joy, protection or warmth that I did. I do not want lies, fear, guilt, shame or betrayal to be a daily part of your lives. Most of all, I want your heart and your soul to stay pure, joyful and full of love for yourself and for others. I would do anything to keep you both from feeling the depths of sorrow and pain that I felt until this moment, until my journey began. I have worked hard at putting the pieces of my heart and soul back together.

In doing so, I have come to realise that I am just as deserving and worthy of love, truth, joy, peace and happiness as the next person. I have realised that I matter. My feelings matter and I deserve to be considered and seen.

So, I have made some really hard decisions, really hard.

A Letter to My Boys

They have been made after doing a lot of work on myself so I can be sure that they have been the right decisions. In making those decisions I have always considered the impact on the both of you and where possible I have tried my hardest to lessen that.

My goal has always been to be the best mother I can be. For me, that means acting consciously, it means accessing the wisdom of my past, it means protecting you and most importantly it means always acting from a place of love and truth.

My wish and dream for us is a future filled with light, joy, laughter, truth, compassion, peace and love. I want you to both be the best you can be, to be who you were born to be. I want your heart to be open and filled with love and I want your soul to sing. I know I will make mistakes along the way, but as long as you grow up knowing that you are loved, protected, nurtured, honoured for who you truly are, then that is all that matters.

I do not regret my past as it has helped to make me who I am today. I have much to be grateful for. In embracing and coming to peace with my past, I hope that neither of you end up carrying it for me.

I love you both so very, very much.

All my love, Mummy

I could not imagine allowing the two little souls that I chose to bring into my life and this world to experience the pain and heartache that I have. Not the normal pain and heartache that life brings, but the type caused by other people who are unable, for their own reasons, to heal their pain – and therefore that pain becomes yours, plus more.

Little did I know that after writing that letter, I would experience deeper heartache, face another tsunami and have my resilience and inner strength tested on many more occasions.

Chapter 14

My Best Friend, Resilience

'What lies behind you and what lies in front of you, pales in comparison to what lies inside of you.'

~ Ralph Waldo Emerson

The years 2009 to 2011 are ones that I would rather skip over, because to revisit them and reflect on all that I endured and came through is overwhelming. I had a two-year-old and a 4½-year-old who would wake every day between 5am and 6am, my family catastrophe occurred and as a result I had no family help. My marriage had broken down and my husband had moved out. I had a casual job, and a house and garden to maintain.

I had a hernia operation two weeks before Christmas and was in hospital for two days – and I then hosted 13 people on Christmas Day, including my ex and his family (I know, WHAT was I thinking?!). We sold our house and I did all of the work for the open for inspections and auction while also negotiating our divorce, including the custody and financial arrangements. We painted three-quarters of the house before selling. The boys and I moved into a rental house. I existed financially fortnight to fortnight and my stress levels sky-rocketed. During this time my husband's grandfather, whom I also considered to be my grandfather, died suddenly.

I sometimes want to shout out to the Universe, 'no more! I understand what resilience is, I am a master now so give me a break!'.

An expression of the anguish I felt during 2009 after my marriage breakdown and family's betrayal

I was beyond exhausted, I was sleep-deprived, and my nervous system and adrenals were fatigued. I fell into old patterns of shutting it all inside and soldiering on. I would count down the hours until my boys would spend the weekend with their dad and I would fall in a heap, trying to recover some part of myself in the two days that they were gone, while attending to household chores and other pressing matters. Could the load have become any heavier? When I look back on the number of major events that occurred within an 18-month timeframe I can only but admire my resilience.

My therapist commented one day that she was surprised I had not had a massive crying meltdown during this period. I can honestly say that some part of me knew that if I allowed myself to release the floodgates I would render myself incapable of looking after my young boys for days. It was a matter of survival, and in some ways my sanity was dependent upon my keeping strong. What did not help is that, often, those tears would start to rise when my boys really needed me, so I would strangle the cry and pull myself together. I recall a couple of times feeling the pressure of the tears as they urged me to let them out – I felt a scream, a primal wail, rising up in my throat, and a deep wanting to express the stress that I felt through every fibre of my being.

It is not that I did not cry at all during this time, but it was controlled. I controlled it and I perpetuated the family pattern of not embracing our feelings, of silencing pain and of pretending to the world that I was coping okay. In truth, I was struggling but I had never been good at asking for help and I did not want to burden anyone with my problems. I stopped calling my friends as I felt I had nothing good to say and, so, what was the point? I shrank within myself and had it not been for my therapist and a couple of other earthly angels, including my two precious boys, I think the nervous breakdown I had narrowly avoided in 2006 would have finally destroyed me.

There was one moment in July 2010, when the boys were at kinder and childcare, when I simply could not contain the emotion. I had just hung up the phone after inquiring into the transfer of my share of the house settlement, which was due to come through that day. I was advised that my share had been put into a trust account that would take another week to be released to me. The lawyer could not do anything. I had less than $100 in the bank, my first monthly rent payment of $1500 was due in four days, I needed to buy groceries to feed the boys and I was not due to be paid for another week. I had nowhere to go, I had no credit card to use and no family to rely on. I collapsed. I fell to my knees on my kitchen floor, sobbing, crying out to God, 'Why? Why do you keep doing this? I cannot take this anymore. Why?'.

I reached out for help – something I had done only a few times in my life. I recalled that my boss had offered to help me out if I ever needed a short-term loan of cash. I felt embarrassed to call her, but call I did, and by the end of the day she had transferred the money for my rent. Some may think that I could have simply paid my rent late, but I did not want to jeopardise the roof over my boys' head – I was their protector and it was up to me to keep them safe. They had also just moved out of the family home and it was important to me that they were secure in this new place.

This experience taught me patience and it confirmed to me that I will always have what I need, even though sometimes I may need to reach out for help – I also know that, by doing so, I am not a failure.

Of course, with hindsight and time to reflect, I should have permitted myself to cry every time the emotion arose so strongly. I realised that I was not saving my boys from anything, anyway. It was foolish of me to think that by not letting my tears fall I was keeping them from knowing the truth about how I felt. They knew I was weeping on the inside. They sensed my pain, and their behaviour simply mirrored what I was not healing or facing.

I would learn to see the boys' behaviour as a signal – if they behaved in a negative way, I realised that I had something that I needed to deal with, within myself. Liam went through a very angry time and I was asked by my therapist, 'What are you angry about?'. At first I said, 'nothing', but being a person who has always self-reflected, I took the time to look within and I admitted to myself that, yes, I was angry. The moment I reached that point, Liam calmed down. His job was done. He had shown me what I could not see in myself and to this day he does the same thing – his anger shows me my anger, although, thankfully, it is a rare occurrence now.

Ultimately, my body began to signal to me that I could not go on the way I was. Firstly, my boys got sick, one after the other, a week at a time. I could not go to work. Then I got sick. It was another moment in time when I knew with all certainty that if I did not change something I was going to end up with a serious illness and then I would be of no use to my boys.

The body is full of wisdom, if we are willing to listen. I had a conversation with my boss about reducing my hours but still I remained sick. Two days later a voice said, 'That was the wrong conversation to have'. So, I resigned, and guess what? My illness disappeared within a day. I had got the message and done what needed to be done. I had been working on healing my mental, emotional and spiritual self and now my body was putting its hand up and saying, 'now it is my turn'.

I made a decision to live off of the money that I received from the house settlement for the following 12 months, and to allow my body to recover from the enormous stresses it had been under. I viewed it as an investment in my future and that of my boys. I viewed it as loving myself enough to say, 'you have been through a great deal and now it is time to nurture and look after yourself'. It was important to me that I be the best mum I could possibly be, and the reality was that I was far from it at that point in time. I simply had nothing left in me to draw on, my patience was wafer-thin and, sensing it, my boys pushed my buttons over and over. What they were really doing was pushing me to deal with my stuff and it was a job well done.

Over those 12 months (which stretched into two years), I would be devoted to putting myself back together physically and emotionally. I invested in massage and energy healings, I took vitamins and supplements, I allowed myself to do things I really wanted to do. I began working with an alchemist, using vibrational essences to help heal my physical and subtle bodies (emotional, etheric, mental, spiritual). Alchemy is not about turning things into gold. It is about working on your inner world so that your outer world starts to transform and reflect the treasure within. I kept Liam in childcare for the first 12 months even though he did not like it and I felt guilty. But I knew that I needed two short days a week to myself in order to come back from the brink of annihilation.

I was so very grateful that we had received a price above the reserve that we had set for our house, for it enabled me to take this time to heal. At the time I placed my trust in myself and the Universe that the future would be okay, and that I would one day get to own a house again if that was what I wanted. The money in the bank would mean nothing if I was seriously ill and unable to care for my boys. Allowing myself to heal has been the most important and valuable investment that I have ever made and will ever make.

Despite all that was going on in my life, my spiritual awakening continued and I would learn much about disconnection and isolation – something I was feeling quite strongly at the time. During this time, I asked myself, 'Why am I so often in a place where no one else is or understands? Why do people have issues with me when I have done or said nothing? Why do I feel like I am a distant participant in life? What is wrong with me? Why do I so often feel like I do not belong?'.

My therapist and spiritual teacher provided me with the insights that I needed. Where there is an absence of love and truth there is disconnection and suffering. My life to that point had lacked truth, so it was no wonder that I'd felt the way I had. It is hard to connect to others and life when two such powerful energies are absent in your world.

Why do we look to others and outside of ourselves for the love, acceptance and validation that we seek? It is in finding self-love and self-acceptance that this disconnection and isolation will slowly disappear and we will attract the right people to us, people who will walk beside us on life's journey.

When it came down to it, it was me and only me who had walked in my shoes, seen with my eyes, felt the anguish, pain and sorrow in my heart, cried my tears, witnessed the events that had shaped me, rallied the strength to keep going and shown the courage to embark on my journey. Finally, I knew in the deepest part of my being how hard I had fought the battle through the

My Best Friend, Resilience

darkness towards the glimmer of light where a life based on joy, peace, love and truth awaited me. It is said we have everything we need within us.

My heart weeps a silent tear,
Can you feel it, anyone near?

Laughter, freedom, love and joy,
A rare and precious gift that I enjoy.

Anguish, sorrow have been my friends,
Please, please tell me when will it end?

In this my darkness, as dark as night,
Begins to shine, a bright and pure golden light.

The pain and sorrow are drifting away,
Love and truth are coming my way.

I have done this – yes, yes, me!
The reward I cannot wait to see.

For my soul has always known,
What I have waited to be shown.

That I am special just as me,
And so now, weary one, let it be.

I survived this period due to the resilience and inner strength that my life had given me up to that point. If it is true that God only gives us what we can handle then my past had prepared me way too well, and even though I know the strength that I have within me, I have no desire for a repeat performance of those challenges. That period stretched me to my limit but ultimately showed me what I was capable of.

This period in my life delivered plenty of lessons that I continue to finetune. When I came out at the other end, I was not the same person. Many people do not understand exactly what I went through, and I am okay with that – for them to understand, they would have to have experienced the same pain, and I would not wish that on anyone. I hope, too, that you can learn a great deal from my own painful experiences without having to go through them for yourself.

For You to Ponder

- What strengths can you identify within yourself?

- Do you hold a belief that it is selfish to put yourself first and take care of your health and wellbeing? If you do, can you identify why? Is this really your belief or is it someone else talking? (That is, have you taken on a pattern or belief from previous generations?)

- What would it feel like to dedicate time to your health and inner wellbeing, your self-care and healing? Close your eyes and let yourself feel what it would be like.

- Reflect on what it would mean to you, your partner or your children for you to invest in your wellbeing. Can you see that it would, in fact, be a gift? (If your cup is full then you have more to give to others.)

Chapter 15
I Heed the Call of a Gallic Song

'To travel is to take a journey into yourself.'

~ Danny Kaye

One of my strengths is following my inner knowing – the voice that whispers to me. It is a feeling of inner peace that settles into my body and I have come to trust it, so I honour it. Reading a magazine in late 2011, my eyes fell upon an ad for a tour. The tour was called 'Journey of the Alchemists' and included Paris, Prague and the south of France. It would be a spiritual journey, where we would be connecting with the Cathars, alchemists, Mary Magdalene and the Black Madonna. In the instant that I saw this ad, I was overcome with excitement, my body tingled and I knew I had to be a part of it.

I had no idea how I would achieve that, as my two boys were only going to be six and 3½ years of age at the time. The tour was also for 23 days. Yet, with a moment of absolute certainty, I was sure it was what I needed to do, that it was crucial to my future and that it would be linked to my purpose, which was yet to reveal itself. On that basis, I simply trusted that it would fall into place and proceeded to arrange for a passport. After talking to the tour host a couple of months later, everything fell into place within the space of a week.

An innocent conversation with someone at my son's Friday gymnastics class resulted in me finding a nanny to do the day shift while I was away, and my ex-husband agreed to come and live at my house and look after the boys for the remainder of the time. I dropped into Flight Centre to enquire about airfares and discovered that it was the last day of a sale, and fares were about to jump up. Every day of that week, the Universe revealed to me in so many ways that I was on the right track. To this very day, I marvel at how many puzzle pieces fell into place to allow me to follow the pull of my soul. It was another moment where I felt truly grateful for the great price we had received on our house sale as it gave me the financial means to go.

Although I knew deep down that I needed to go, I was worried about leaving my boys behind for that length of time. But I also sensed that they were going to be okay. A tribe of people were in place, I had filled the freezer with their favourite meals and I had created a poster with words of love and a photo of me that they put beside their bed.

On the day of my flight in May 2012, we all had on our brave faces but my heart ached at saying goodbye to those gorgeous boys. As the plane took off, I had a vision of all the people who had encouraged me to go and had stepped in to help holding me up and sending me off with love. It was a vision that made me cry.

I knew from early on that I needed to have a single room so that I could be in silence each night, processing what would happen during the day. It was one of the smartest decisions I could have made. This tour was about my personal growth and I wanted to get as much out of it as I could. I confess that my priority was not to make great friends and I felt it was important that I kept some distance so as not to get caught up in any drama or in other people's 'stuff'. If I was leaving my boys behind for so long I wanted to make it worth it.

The three weeks that followed were simply life-changing. France had called to me for a reason. My soul had come home again, but this time there was work to do – that work would sow the seeds of my business and my purpose, which germinated six months later.

Apart from working with an alchemist here in Melbourne as part of my healing, I had had no connection with or interest in the other elements of the tour. I had never heard of the Cathars. Being raised a Catholic I knew of Mary Magdalene (only from the highly politicised and patriarchal viewpoint) but had never heard of the Black Madonna. Despite that, I was intrigued by it all and I soaked up every experience, every feeling, every bit of information and history that was shared. Stories of the Knights

Templar, Nicholas Flamel and other alchemists in Paris and Prague fascinated me. I could not get enough. (If you're curious to know more about the Cathars, Mary Magdalene and the Black Madonna, I have reading recommendations for you in the 'Feed Your Mind & Soul' chapter later in this book.)

I loved being back in Prague, a beautiful city that escaped the destruction of World War II, and I discovered another layer and aspect of its history. Of course, I am always happy to return to Paris. We had the first Sunday of our tour free, and four of us spent the day walking through the streets, strolling beside the Seine, chatting, stopping for lunch, and resting under the blossom trees at the base of the Eiffel Tower, eating the new season cherries we had purchased at the market that morning.

I felt like a local, spending my Sunday out in that beautiful city, a destination in mind but the journey to get there spontaneous and flowing. We ended our 10-hour day of walking with a delicious dinner in a local bistro – hearty French food and a glass of red wine. That day was a highlight of the tour for me.

Heading south from Paris and visiting Chartres Cathedral for the first time, I was overcome with emotion as I stood under the South Portal Rose window. It is one of the most beautiful cathedrals I have ever entered, and it is a deeply spiritual place. I felt I had been there before. I would make a promise to fulfil my purpose as I sat in a pew, weeping.

Much further south, in Rocamadour, I communed with the

Black Madonna, following guidance that I was, three times, to visit the Basilica where she resides. I knew not for what purpose, but obey that guidance, I did. The Basilica hosts a shrine dedicated to the Virgin Mary and was once one of the most famous pilgrim sites in the whole of Christianity. Throughout Europe, there are many Black Madonnas that date from medieval times (the 12th to 15th centuries). There are suggestions that they relate to the worship of goddesses such as Isis.

We then travelled further south to the town of Carcassonne, in the Languedoc region. It was here that the story of the Cathars (who existed from the 12th century to the early 14th century) was unveiled. Ever since knowledge of their existence had entered my world, I had been intrigued. I felt a deep connection to this area in the south-west of France – in particular the Languedoc and Midi-Pyrenees regions – and my intuition told me that I was, indeed, returning home.

The story of the Cathars (from a Greek word meaning 'the pure ones') and their persecution is fascinating, tragic and worth reading about. They were a peaceful group who did not believe that you needed to attend church or revere a statue to be close to God. Women were allowed to be spiritual leaders, as they were believed to be equally as capable as men. Love was at the heart of their beliefs and some say they were descendants of Mary Magdalene. However, it needs to be said that there is a great deal of conjecture about the true nature of their beliefs, because much of what was written was penned by enemies, and possibly misunderstood. In the year 1208 they were deemed to be heretics, and Pope Innocent III called for a crusade – it was known as the Albigensian Crusade. For more than a century the crusades and subsequent inquisitions inflicted great tragedy and loss on the Cathars, all but eradicating them by 1321. Whole towns were massacred, believers were burnt at the stake, and blood and persecution stained the land.

For five days we toured Cathar castles and ruins, braving bitterly cold days, rain and wind; the rivers swollen and raging with the recent snow melt. Stunning scenery, haunting and abandoned ruins. The place that has stayed with me ever since is Montségur. This was where more than 220 Cathars were burnt at the stake on 16 March 1244, following a siege that lasted for months and a two-week truce where they had to decide whether to renounce their beliefs or die – to be burnt alive at the stake. On that day, they would walk together down the mountain, prepared to die for what they believed in.

Sitting on the hillside of Montségur, I imagined that I would feel the grief of those who had watched their loved ones die all those centuries ago. What I felt instead was deep and profound. As I looked towards the snow-capped Pyrenees in the distance, breathing in the majesty and beauty of the forested mountains against a backdrop of a clear and blue sky, I felt for sure that I was at a place where heaven and earth met. I felt the presence of God.

I Heed the Call of a Gallic Song

I could have sat there on my rock, the wildflowers surrounding me, staring at that view and breathing in the divine essence of that special place for the whole day. I felt at peace and I felt loved. I vowed that one day I would return and sit upon that hillside for as long as I wanted, drawing the magnetic power of Montségur into my heart once more.

When we travelled to Provence, I learned of an old Provençal legend that said that Mary Magdalene had arrived on the shores at Saintes Marie de la Mer, having fled the unrest following the crucifixion and resurrection of Jesus. The legend states that she spent the remaining 30 years of her life in a cave in the Forest of Baume. When I visited this forest, I felt, for the first time, that there was something invisible around me. I could feel its presence and its energy but could not see it. My experiences in the forest and cave would mark the beginning of a connection with Mary that continues to this day.

When I sat down on a pew in the cave, I asked Mary if she had a message for me. Immediately and unexpectedly she began to share a long message that I somehow remembered, despite not having pen and paper on me. In one part of the message she kept repeating, 'You know the way, you know the way'. Well, at that moment I didn't feel that I knew the way or what she was referring to. When I shared this with the tour host, she mentioned something about early (pre-) Christianity being known as The Way.

As it turned out, it was the elements that I had not been

connected to, prior to the tour – namely the Black Madonna, the Cathars and Mary Magdalene – that would bring about the life-changing moments that I experienced on the tour. They are also the elements that have, in fact, continued to unveil more and more to me since that journey. Although, what role they are to play in my life is as yet unclear, but I am excited about watching it all unfold. Much of what I learned simply blew my mind. I drank it in eagerly and I felt the truth of the words that were shared by the tour hosts, or those I read in guidebooks and leaflets, within my own body. The energy I felt from these places also supported this truth.

There is far too much for me to share in the space of this book, suffice it to say that during my journey through France I received many messages and guidance about the path I was to walk, and that path revealed my business and my purpose. With no plans to run my own tour, I recall noting all the things I would do differently, and the things that could make a person's experience even more special.

Little did I know that, later that year on a glorious spring day, while enjoying a French-inspired picnic in Williamstown Botanic Gardens, my dear friend Susanne would suggest that I run my own tour to France. I would receive my own intuitive confirmation (I receive goosebumps or tingles all over my body) that this was exactly what I was to do. It goes to show that, deep down, your heart and soul always knows the perfect path for you and is guiding you in every moment – even if you do not know why at the time.

I had been propelled onto a new trajectory and it would open me up for even more healing, surrendering and letting go. France had called. I had heeded that call and a path had opened up for me that I excitedly began to journey down. There was no turning back now.

For You to Ponder

- In the past, have you responded to a yearning or calling of your heart to do something? If so, can you see how the Universe supported you in making it happen?

- Is there now a yearning or calling of your heart that you keep ignoring? If so, why are you ignoring it? Can you trust in the Universe to support you in making it happen?

Chapter 16

Learning to Love & Accept Myself

'If I am not good to myself, how can I expect anyone else to be good to me?'

~ Maya Angelou

Following my journey to France, which I call my personal pilgrimage, I began a period of discovering more about who I really am and learning to love and accept me, with all my strengths and weaknesses, flaws and gifts. I found that some aspects were easy to accept, while others took more work and involved layers of healing.

As a result, I became better at observing myself, although I would have moments in the next two years where I was tested and where I then crumbled. But I was okay with that, as I needed to crumble in order to learn and let go – so that more of who I am could be revealed.

During this time, I had particular themes that arose for me. One of the first was vulnerability. A friend of mine told me about Brené Brown's TED talk on vulnerability, and I loved it. Two quotes that I love from the TED talk are:

'Vulnerability is our most accurate measurement of courage.'

'Vulnerability is not weakness. And that myth is profoundly dangerous.'

How many of us do believe that we are weak if we are vulnerable? After listening to Brené's talk, I knew I had to look at myself and ask, 'Am I afraid to be vulnerable? Is that fear holding me back from living life fully?'. After much reflection, it was clear that I was afraid to be vulnerable, especially in the context of not being protected against emotional hurt.

I had been guided to start a business that helps women to tap into their divine feminine essence and for them to see the innate power in doing so. For me, the divine feminine essence is about living from the heart; it is about love and inner strength; it is life force. It is about creativity, feeling, embracing your body, wisdom, going with the flow, faith and nurturing. The idea is not to lose your connection to your masculine essence of living from the mind, of attaining goals, doing, willpower, direction, understanding or insight. While, as women, we mostly embody the feminine essence, it is about finding a healthy balance, because everyone contains both feminine and masculine qualities within them.

Starting a new business where I was putting my views on 'women' and 'the feminine' out into the world was scary. I was exposed and there was a feeling of real vulnerability. Would people listen to what I had to say? Would I be persecuted for standing up and speaking my truth? Would I lose friends who might find my truth uncomfortable or confronting? Would anyone turn up to events that I organised? Would my boys pay the price for me speaking out?

Once I started my business – originally called The Way of the Feminine – I had to address all of these things. I would struggle with some of them for quite a while, but I knew that the option of not following through with my life's purpose was far more of a risk than exposing myself to any emotional hurt caused by speaking my truth. For me, there was simply no choice.

During this time, I began a new relationship for the first time since my marriage ended five years prior. Those vulnerability buttons were pushed, big time. I felt I had done a great deal of work on myself both before and after my divorce (and continued to do so) and I knew I was ready to give my heart to someone.

However, until you are again in a relationship of some meaning, there is no way of knowing how ready you are to be truly vulnerable. It's a real test to open your heart fully, to allow yourself to love, to let go, to experience all the joy that a new relationship offers without fear of the outcome, or fear of being hurt.

For the most part, I was open and allowing. However, I could feel that that wall of protection was still there, although it was not as big or as thick as it used to be. But it still existed, and an internal battle raged on. Will I have my heart broken again? If I love again will someone love me? If I love I will lose control over my life. The wall allowed me to control but it also meant my whole being was not invested or, indeed, available.

After much reflection and soul searching, I knew that for me to have the relationship I had dreamed of, the one that was the light of hope in times of darkness, I would have to allow myself to be vulnerable. To remove that wall and open my heart to the possibilities, despite my fear, without knowing the outcome, without any guarantees. To just relax and allow this good thing into my life to blossom and grow. For when I stopped allowing past hurts to control me, when I made myself vulnerable, surrendered to love and opened my heart, it felt really good. I had made a vow to myself that my life would be lived from the heart – this was one area where I would keep that promise, despite the fear.

Along my journey to self-love and self-acceptance, one of the hardest things I've dealt with has been freeing myself from the endless chatter of my mind, and the fear and doubt that has been its song. Part of the process of accepting myself as I am has been realising that one of my true demons is my mind.

As I worked through layers and layers of pain and gunk in order to try to release myself from the feeling of being trapped, of being caged in a life I instinctively knew was not all it could be, it became apparent that what was still trapping me was my own mind. Yes, I was the person trying to free myself but I was also the one keeping myself bound tight, protected, secure (or so I thought) from further pain and sorrow.

Oh, I would be positive and upbeat for a period of time and I could picture a life that represented who I really am but then in flowed the story, the fear and the doubts. A little demon sitting on my shoulder, the voice in my head saying, 'No, it is just going to be the same. Nothing good will last. Those things cannot happen to you. You will just sabotage it anyway. What do you have to say that people will want to listen to? You do not deserve that. Why would someone love you?'. Wow! Would I say those things out loud to another person, to someone I loved? Would I even say those things to a stranger? Never!

So it was that I would decide that I had had enough. It was time to take control of this demon, instead of it controlling me. I was ready to scream, frustrated and so 'over' getting in my own way. Why exactly could I *not* have all that I dreamed of? Why did I need to delay stepping into that dream by keeping myself bound – for no good reason? Why did I not feel that I deserved an amazing life? Why could I not talk to myself in a loving and kind way? Why would I allow this self-inflicted suffering to continue?

It was almost as though the Universe was presenting me with a challenge. How much do you want to live a life of love, passion, abundance and joy while expressing the truth of who you really are? If you really want it, are you going to let your mind and the voices of fear and doubt win? If you really want it, you are going to have to fight to control it and you are going to have to practise daily, in every moment, holding the vision for your life in your heart. This quote from Oprah would help me:

'I believe that every single event in life that happens is an opportunity to choose love over fear.'

~ Oprah Winfrey

When those voices arise – the ones based on my past – I now say to myself over and over, 'No, that is not part of my story anymore. I deserve it and am worthy'. I have become an observer of my thoughts and I use my journal to help record them and work through them. I see them as an opportunity to release old beliefs and create more loving and kind thoughts. For I have learned over the years that you cannot run away from your mind so you might as well face it and deal with it.

Of course, it has not been an easy task, turning the mind into my servant. It is still very much a work in progress and there are days when the mind takes control. However, day by day, I will myself to win this battle. I am determined that all of the work I have done on my inner world is not going to be sabotaged anymore by a mind that is limited and wants to keep me stuck in the past, instead of being a co-author of a new story. No, my dream life is waiting for me; I am waiting for me to step up and arrive fully in my life. Only I can free myself from that which binds, only I can love myself and deem myself worthy enough to say, 'you deserve it all and more'.

During this time of learning to love and accept myself, I would also make peace with my body. I have felt so self-conscious of my body for much of my life. When I was much younger I wore a T-shirt over my one piece swimsuit to hide myself, although, when I reflect back 20-odd years ago, I remember that I was a size 8 to 10 (Australian)! I thought I did not have the body to wear a bikini or to even strut my stuff in a one piece.

I would look at all the women on the beach, the different shapes and sizes, and marvel at their confidence in being comfortable with their bodies. I wondered why I had so much trouble with mine. I always wanted to buy and wear a bikini but never could bring myself to.

As I have worked to reconnect to the feminine part of me over the last few years, I have discovered that I now love wearing dresses, I wear make-up more often and I am happy to show my curves. Last year I began the process of wearing a bikini – albeit, I was still covered up but I did buy one, and I wore it.

However, at the beginning of this year, I decided to take the plunge. I felt great in a bikini, sexy even, and I challenged myself to wear it loud and proud down at the beach. I did – and guess what? The sky did not fall down, people's eyes did not burn at the sight of me and life went on as normal. Surprise, surprise. It was my first big achievement for 2015.

I am proud to embrace this body of mine with its cellulite, its untoned muscles and its stretch marks. This body has carried me for the last 44 years, given birth naturally to two children, carried another for a short time, been in car accidents, fallen from trees, endured hours of fitness work when I was obsessed with netball, moved heavy boxes countless times, supported my backpack for months as I travelled Europe, and more. This body has carried all of my emotional pain, and my organs have supported me and kept me breathing when I thought I could not go on. This body is the vessel for my soul and I am proud of it.

My body is a living testament to my life as a woman. I am not going to be ashamed of my body anymore and I am not concerned with how others may view it, for they do not know how much my body has served me and done for me. I do not care what the magazines, the tabloids or the million 'experts' tell me about how I should look in a bikini. I am the only person who matters and I feel good – in fact, great – in a bikini.

Learning to love and accept myself has been a long process and continues to be something on which I work. It has involved really understanding who I am and being okay with that.

I understand that I live my life from my heart and that my intuition/knowing/inner voice has always been there and is something I can trust and rely on. That when I follow that intuition, magic happens, my life flows, I am where I need to be, doing what I need to be doing. I understand that I am an introvert and that not having a huge circle of friends or a packed social calendar is okay.

I understand that I choose not to walk the same path as a lot of people. I understand that I take responsibility for my part in any situation, and self-reflect, always. I accept that I need to honour who I am and how I walk through life, for to deny it is to deny my truth.

With this newfound understanding and acceptance of myself, I have given up the self-induced suffering, the need for acceptance by others, the need to fit in, and the need to explain myself, my decisions or my way of being. I have severed my attachment to the story, to the past and to outdated beliefs.

Breaking free of that which binds me has allowed me to honour my truth and live my life from my heart, always. My hope is that I continue to do it with much grace and gratitude for all that has been, for all those who have gone before and for all that unfolds in the future. Loving, accepting and understanding myself has brought me inner peace and great freedom and that alone is a treasure worth seeking.

I wish the same for you – that you, too, will find the inner peace and freedom that comes with loving, accepting and understanding yourself. There is an exercise on the next page, in this chapter's 'For You to Ponder' section, that helps you to achieve this for yourself. The treasure is within you, always.

For You to Ponder

In this chapter, I shared many questions that I posed to myself as I journeyed along the path towards self-love and self-acceptance. I invite you to read back through this chapter and to reflect on those same questions in terms of *you* and how you feel about yourself, your life and your experiences.

Consider journaling your responses, and returning in a year and asking yourself the same questions, to see how much you have grown.

Following are two extra exercises that you can explore to deepen your love and acceptance of yourself:

- I encourage you to view your body as the sacred vessel that is the home for your soul. Can you see how it has supported you along your own journey? Can you love and appreciate your body for that support, despite any judgements you may have about how it looks? Find at least one thing to love about your body.

- Close your eyes and sit quietly. Imagine that you see a reflection of yourself standing before you. In your imagination, step forward and hug yourself tightly. Express gratitude to your reflection for having the courage to consider the questions in this chapter for yourself; for having the courage to begin the journey of loving and accepting who you are; for beginning your journey home to your real treasure; for the strength and wisdom you hold in your own heart; for the love and nurturing you give to others; for opening your heart to the infinite possibilities that are available to you. For the amazing woman that you already are.

Chapter 17
A Heart Cracked Open

'New beginnings are often disguised as painful endings.'

~ Lao Tzu

Whenever I dare to think that I have made it through my stuff, that I am done and finished, the Universe decides to show me otherwise. Ha! If there was ever a year to show me that healing and evolving is an ongoing process, then 2014 was it. My second tsunami had arrived.

I had enrolled in a Certificate of Holistic Counselling course that began in February 2014 and went for nine months. I never enrolled with the intention of becoming a counsellor; rather, to use the skills and tools on my tours and in my workshops, should they be required. I also sensed that the course was the next puzzle piece of my healing journey.

I knew with absolute certainty that I had to do the course. I had looked into enrolling a couple of years prior and had found it interesting but I clearly had not felt ready. When I received the newsletter advising that course enrolments were open, I booked and paid on the spot. I had no idea of what I was about to embark upon, other than the fact that I kept getting the word 'family' whenever I thought about the course. I also felt that I was ready to delve into the next layer of healing. Sometimes I think that, perhaps, I should have taken a moment to really ponder on whether or not I was up for it! The course began on 14 February. This would also be the day that my first post-marriage relationship began a catastrophic descent into nothingness.

So began a year where I witnessed and felt the depths of my inner being in a way that I never thought I would. On the first weekend of my course I got a taste of what I was in for, and I was so not prepared. We were introduced to the concept of Family Constellations – this is a process that seeks to reveal the hidden dynamics of your relationship or family. It is experiential in nature and can help to dissolve often-destructive family patterns. It's a gentle method of allowing a resolution to unfold through the exposing of family or relationship energy via representatives in a workshop format, or with props in a private one-on-one session. (If you'd like to know more about Family Constellations, I have included some links in the 'Feed Your Mind & Soul' chapter at the end of this book.)

During that first weekend, I experienced a profound and life-changing transformation that reached into my soul. It unleashed a dam of tears that nothing else had been able to trigger on my journey. That dam was clearly overflowing and the pressure valve had been released. The saying, 'crying your tears is cleansing your soul' never felt so real or true for me.

Over that weekend, I gained insights into my family and an understanding that would form the basis of the deeper compassionate perspective I would gain in the months to follow. But, in that moment of transformation, where time did not exist, where I have never felt so present, I was able to hand back so much of what my mother and my grandmother had unconsciously asked me to carry for them throughout my life. Afterwards, I lay down, exhausted, and was held in a safe embrace by one of the facilitators. I shook for 20 minutes. I released from my body, my muscles and my cells trauma that had frozen me and kept me trapped all my life. The area around my stomach felt so much lighter and within a week I would notice that I had lost weight, which I have never put back on. A weight had literally been lifted and it demonstrated how food and diets are not always the reason why our weight will not shift.

After that experience, I tried to recover physically and emotionally – however, 12 days later I had the rug pulled out from underneath me. My boyfriend ended our relationship for good. His own story, pain and entanglements were becoming a barrier for him; he had decided that he was not good enough for me and needed to spend time sorting himself out. I instinctively knew that this was true for him, and all I could do was just let him go. Despite this inner knowing, I fell to my knees, devastated and in shock, barely able to speak, and into the arms of my soul sister Kimberley, who would be my rock and my anchor in the months to come.

Nothing seemed to make sense. We had been planning a future together, and were at a place where we had reached a deeper level. Clearly, this had been the trigger for his pain and he no longer wished to hurt me or allow that pain to be projected onto me. He was not ready to step up and follow his words with actions.

I spent the best part of the next year trying to comprehend what had happened, why my intuition and inner knowing had seemed to be so 'off'. Trying to understand what God was teaching me and questioning why it had to be so excruciatingly painful. Why had we been brought together, with both of us feeling that we had found 'it'? Why, when we had a connection that felt beyond the heart and came from the soul, were we so far apart now? Why? Why? Why? My journal was the place where I poured forth my agony and my devastation. I sought understanding from tarot readers and psychics when I asked for a sign from the Universe. I turned to my healing team again to help me.

My course would plunge me into deeper experiences, with a second powerful Family Constellation session bringing a release and healing that I had never expected. It enabled me to gain a greater understanding around the effects of my brother's death and my resulting disconnection from my mother. With the encouragement of the facilitator, I felt a force within me rise up from my core, a force that erupted with the power of a volcano. A primal rage contained within it all the anger, frustration and feelings that I had never expressed out of loyalty and a misguided sense of love. The rage was released out of my mouth and directed at my mother. The heat I felt in my body was astounding and it reflected the sheer amount of energy that I had just discharged. Again, I lay down exhausted, raw but freed, then falling asleep and resting my soul.

One of the saddest moments I experienced during the course was in a meditation, when we first visualised our inner child. The vision of my inner child was of a small malnourished girl aged six. She was serious, lacking life, lonely, drab and dirty. What I understood was that when she shows up in me she feels overwhelmed, isolated and lonely. She told me that she wanted me to practise self-love and -care and to honour that little girl. I could see that if I did, my inner child would fill out, have colour in her cheeks, and would be clean, smiling and beautiful.

Now, when I feel overwhelmed, I realise it is my inner child trying to get my attention. It is then time to connect with her and ask her what she needs. I talk to her and tell her she is safe now that we are in control of how things work out. I tell her that we have all that we need.

With both the course and my relationship breakdown, I was challenged, pushed and plunged into my deepest heart wounds. For months my heart literally hurt, as if someone had plunged a knife into the very core and was cutting it up, bit by bit. My chest felt as if it was being prised open.

At some points throughout that year I seriously do not know how I managed to get on with my life. I could not talk about my relationship breakdown due to the pain. I also had to get myself into a space where I understood what had happened and could therefore answer any questions that others asked of me. I was lucky to have a small group of friends who knew and who patiently allowed me to process, weep, grieve and find my way out of the abyss. They allowed me to do it in my own way, trusting that I knew what was right for me but also sharing their concern and their insights. These women held me up and never let go. They were the vessel that caught my tears and the pain that oozed out of me.

The course gave me a deeper understanding of how pain is passed on through generations, and why. I learned that not everything was my responsibility. I learned that everyone has a story, and what goes on in a relationship or exchange often has nothing to do with you. I learned of how I was projecting onto others, how I had not yet healed all the pain from my marriage, how I did not really trust, how I was protecting my heart from further heartache (well, that had worked well!). I learned that everyone has a natural place in your family, based on when they joined (by birth, marriage, adoption, conception, partnership and so on) and so I honoured my miscarriage and now talk about my three children. Within me, a tree of compassion grew for my family.

In the course I unwrapped another layer of my femininity, and found that I loved resting in that space. This unwrapping occurred in particular on the 'Love, Sex and Relationships' weekend, where we delved into our inner feminine and masculine. We learned ways to strengthen both of these essences; we connected to our body by evoking our senses; and we discovered ways to open up the body and awaken our sexual energy (to me, sexual energy is life force – not just the physical act of sex). I let go of beliefs and thoughts that no longer served me. I discovered that I was so ready to move beyond my past and my story. I was ready to start writing a new narrative with an entirely different plot and characters.

The end of my relationship taught me lessons that bring me only gratitude. I learned that love means allowing someone to walk their own journey, in their own way, even if it means that they leave you behind. I learned that I could not control the outcome of everything in my life. I learned that sometimes love is not enough to save a relationship – in fact, sometimes love is the reason that it ends. I learned that I could not rescue someone from themselves or save them from their own pain. I learned to be humble.

My boyfriend had awakened my sensuality and I felt desired and like a woman for the first time in my life. This alone was deeply healing for me, as I had thought for many years that there was something wrong with me when it came to sex. No, in order for that aspect of me to awaken I had just been waiting for the right man and the right circumstances. The power of sexuality when you share such a deep and soulful connection is something I wish for every woman. Sex with someone where that connection is not present does not hold the same appeal anymore. I have felt what it's possible to experience and there is no going back. He pushed me to open my heart to unconditional love – true, unconditional love. I learned what it was like to rest in the embrace of masculine strength and to allow my own masculine to rest.

Following the break-up, the most difficult thing for me was untangling myself from the soul connection. Knowing that on a spirit level we are always connected, but that in our human form the time was not right for us to be together. I know deep within me that we have not fulfilled the promise we made together in this life, that we have unfinished business. But that is okay. We all have choices in every moment whether to stay on the path or to deviate, whether to return, or to keep walking further away. I have accepted his choice, I have thanked him in a letter and I have expressed gratitude to his face for all that he taught me and gave me. I wish him only happiness.

It is impossible within the space of this book to share the depths of learning and understanding that I gained as a result of losing my soul mate and, in some ways, it's too soon for me to put pen to paper. But one day I will as I do not believe that I went through that experience to stay silent and not share the wisdom that I acquired.

Through all of my experiences in 2014, I learned in a much more conscious way how to take the pain and suffering one is feeling and turn it into wisdom and gold. It was a year when all the hurts and rivers of pain – which had been held in a cavern deep inside for decades – bled out, transforming my heart and making space for new experiences, joy, love and abundance.

My holistic counselling course and relationship breakdown taught me that sometimes love means walking away or letting someone go, even though it may not be what you want. I learned that it is not for me to judge the path that someone has chosen to walk for themselves in this lifetime, and by trying to rescue them I may, in fact, be denying them the opportunity to awaken and free themselves. It was not up to me to decide what was best for someone else. Hadn't the wisdom I had obtained been revealed in my own moments of darkness?

Those experiences have enabled me to start writing a new story for myself, one that is created from my heart, reflecting who I am without anyone else's stuff blocking and crippling me. The darkness and pain that I so willingly agreed to carry for others has been transformed into a shining light. A new way of being is what awaits me now – I am humbled, calm and centred.

I am finally ready to love big and love fearlessly.

My heart feels free, purged, unburdened and cracked open, bursting with life and love, ready to receive love and ready to give love in a much more expanded and real way. However, I will never again compromise myself or beg someone to love me. If they want to love me, they can step up and show me. Love and light proved to be the ultimate guideposts in a year that took me to the limits of my strength and courage. Light and love would now guide me home.

For You to Ponder

- Are you a rescuer, like I was?

- Do you allow yourself to be vulnerable in your relationships, work or everyday life?

- Are you allowing past hurts to hold you back from fully experiencing love in a new relationship?

- Are you projecting your fear of being hurt again onto a new partner (in the way that I did)?

- I encourage you to evoke your senses and awaken your sensuality – see the 'For You to Delve Deeper...' chapter later in this book for ideas on how to do this.

Chapter 18
Creating a New Melody

*'A woman in harmony with her spirit
is like a river flowing.
She goes where she will without pretense
and arrives at her destination
prepared to be herself
and only herself.'*

~ Maya Angelou

In May 2014, with my heart breaking, I took steps towards fulfilling a dream. I began composing the notes of my new melody by flying to Paris to research a tour I had developed for women – the tour that my friend Susanne had suggested, on our springtime picnic under an azure blue sky, in late 2012. I had 16 days by myself in Paris and Provence and, now, after months of researching and planning, it was time to begin my journey.

Flying out to France, I was exhausted, in need of some distance from my everyday life and in need of space to just be. I wanted to connect even more deeply to my feminine essence, to live from my heart every day and to banish, just for a short time, the tendency to let my head get in the way. I had an itinerary to research and test but I also wanted to allow myself to be in the flow and to allow my soul to guide me.

I had not travelled by myself for this length of time before. I was a little anxious about how I would go, despite having been to France many times before. However, I knew I had it in me, so once my feet hit the ground in Paris I took a deep breath and said to myself, 'just stay calm... allow yourself to be guided... and all will be okay'.

During my time in Paris I would wake up with a sense of what I needed to achieve that day, but I allowed myself the flexibility to be led astray. My inner voice popped up every now and then and guided me – go down this street, ask this person for directions, go inside this door – and trusting always.

By doing this, so many beautiful experiences opened up for me. Some were very small, some were personal and some related to the tour. When I found myself in a moment of magic, I stayed present, breathing in the smells, sounds, sights and feelings. I expressed gratitude for Spirit talking to me directly, or through other people.

I had many moments like this on my trip. My days flowed. I had no time restrictions, I listened to my heart and my inner voice and things fell into place. I realise now that my feminine was alive. It was the way I want to live every day of my life – allowing, listening, trusting and loving. I experienced joy and magic. I felt at one with life. Not resisting and not fearing. I believed in my abilities and in myself.

The exhilaration of seeing the Eiffel Tower again, the beauty of the gardens, the architecture, and history on every corner… all proved to be the perfect tonic for my aching heart. I savoured the taste of a warm *pain au chocolat*, lining up with the locals at 7.30am to wait for the boulangerie to open. When I was greeted with a smile and 'bonjour' from the men cleaning the streets in the early morning, I returned that smile, seeing the pride that they had for this beautiful city.

I wandered along the historic streets of the Marais district on Sunday, stopping to listen to bands playing on the pavement, observing the families who were lunching and strolling. I sat in the window of a small café early one morning, the soft sound of jazz music in the background, the waiter in his white shirt and black vest allowing me to practise my French numbers when it was time to pay. I walked and walked, researching, tasting, discovering, refining. As I walked, I healed.

In Provence, I stayed in a gorgeous renovated Provençal townhouse in the village of St Remy de Provence. The townhouse was owned by Tim and Jenny, an English couple who reside in a village nearby. Here, I slowed down, although my days were filled with driving and exploring, working out what was to be included in the tour and what did not fit with the experience I wanted to create. I visited hilltop villages, markets, restaurants,

Roman ruins, gardens, museums and more, driven and guided by Tim. I practised my limited French, shopped at the local market, braved the stern French lady to buy goat cheese, and walked in the Alpilles Mountains amongst the wild thyme and rosemary with Jenny. I made wonderful connections with people who will help me bring the dream of this tour alive and I allowed the spirit of the land to envelope me and embrace me.

Something happened for me on that trip that had never happened before in France (or anywhere, for that matter). Arriving back in Paris from Provence, I was passing through turnstiles at a Metro station when my bag, which I was pulling behind me, became stuck. I stood there looking around, not knowing what on earth to do. I could not pull it through. Then, as if by magic, four Frenchmen ran towards me and began to push and pull my bag. I stood there, helpless, worried that they were going to break my bag. I said in English, 'Please do not break my bag'. Despite their strength and valiant efforts the bag would not budge. Then, along came the thinking man with his ticket – he swiped it and the turnstile opened! I thanked them all in my limited French, and one of the men then proceeded to carry my bag for me, down the stairs to the platform. I felt spoiled.

I laughed to myself as I walked away. It was the first time in my life that I had ever been a damsel in distress. In fact, it was the first time that I had allowed myself to be a damsel in distress. I realised that the reason the men came running is because I did not project an energy that said, 'It is fine, I can do it, I am quite capable and I do not need your help'.

On that trip I felt 'seen' as a woman for the first time in my life and, trust me, I had been to France before and not felt it. Apart from the damsel episode, I had a number of other experiences that contributed to this feeling. Simply walking along the street and having a man smile at you. Having the table of old Frenchmen in Le Bistrot du Paradou invite Jenny (my host in St Remy de Provence) and myself to join them. So many little nuances all helped to make my feminine come alive and dance for joy even more. It was very healing for me and I loved it.

Every day of that visit to France was a chance for me to create a melody that would not only bring *me* joy, but bring joy to women all over the globe. A melody created from my heart, with love as its essence. I had never felt so connected to my purpose, my soul or my passion. France provided my heart and soul a refuge. I believe that France is a place of beauty, alive with the essence of the feminine. It is the place where I feel most at peace, and connected to my heart. I also believe it is no accident that Paris is called the City of Love and Light. When I arrive in France, I always feel as though I have come home – and on that visit the new melody that I was composing became clearer and sweeter.

For You to Ponder

- Can you begin to let go of parts of your old story? To start creating new chapters and storylines that feature different outcomes to what you have experienced in the past?

- I invite you to see yourself as the composer of your own melody. To see that you have all the power and resources you need within you to create a new tune. Can you see that you have the power to do this for yourself?

- Is there something that you have always wanted to do, but you keep ignoring it and pushing it aside? For example, to travel, to write, to create, or to start your own business? What is stopping you from doing it? Are there limiting beliefs or issues you need to address in order to let yourself do the thing that you have always wanted to do? Can this longed-for activity or experience form part of your new melody?

Chapter 19
Taking Flight

*'When I let go of what I am,
I become what I might be.'*

~ Lao Tzu

I launched my business – originally called The Way of the Feminine – on 8 March 2013, which was International Women's Day. I was excited, full of ideas and passionate about what I wanted to achieve. I believe that we should celebrate our achievements and important milestones in life, so I chose to 'walk my talk' by celebrating the launch surrounded by those who loved and supported me.

When I created my business, I knew that, as a woman, I am not alone in many of my experiences. My passion was then, and still very much is, to connect women back to the treasure contained within. To connect them so that they can finally take a deep breath and love the beautiful woman that they already are but have perhaps never accepted or acknowledged. This book is just one way that I am fulfilling that purpose.

Connected to my passion for helping women is a very strong desire to help young girls. The experiences of my childhood resulted in me disconnecting from my dreams, my true beauty and my heart. They triggered a loss of confidence and a loss of self-belief. I know the profound impact that an unhappy childhood can have on a woman's life, and my experiences have fuelled a passion within me to provide a way for young girls to nourish their inner health and wellbeing. My deepest hope is that they grow up without chains around their legs or their throat, stopping them from soaring and achieving their fullest potential or from voicing their truth. Imagine what they could achieve if they are not crippled by all that has held so many of us down?

Since the warm autumn evening of my business launch, I have had small successes with some of my ideas and great enthusiasm for others that ultimately did not work out. I have had to postpone and revise, and, as a result, try to not fall in a hole, feeling like a failure. I have assessed what I am really passionate about and I have chosen to focus on what brings me alive inside. Where I know I can bring the best of me, with my intention firmly based in my heart. Only when I sing from my soul and my heart do I know that I can make a difference.

I have dealt with my own self-sabotage born out of a fear of being successful, a fear of not being good enough, a fear of having my voice heard and whether, indeed, I have anything valuable to say. On those days when I do not seem to be getting anywhere, I have doubted whether I should continue.

My healing journey did not stop during the creation of my business, and that journey continues. I have come to realise that all of the inner work that I have done has been necessary and crucial, enabling me to hold a loving space for all the women and girls whom I serve. To be able to be authentic, compassionate and true, I have needed to have faced my own pain and heart wounds, and accept responsibility for what I co-created in my work, relationships and friendships – for it is never one-sided, no matter how much we want to point the finger and lay blame on others.

Eighteen months after I launched my business, I finally felt as though I was truly in a place where I was ready to take my vision and passion out into the wider world. To see it blossom, grow and thrive. It was time to step out beyond the close circle that, in reality, was keeping me safe.

I exhibited at my first expo in the spring of 2014. I loved connecting with all of those who stopped by. I felt energised talking about my passion and I received some great feedback. The world began to open up. I felt like the bud that has been asleep all winter, waiting for the right time to start growing and blossoming into the beautiful flower that nature intended.

However, I was then drawn to exhibit at another, larger expo, to be held five months later. In a moment of madness I had booked a spot to speak on the main stage for 30 minutes. What was I thinking?! My inner knowing sensed that this expo was a game-changer, a turning point.

My ego obviously sensed it, too, and it went into overdrive. Just days before I was to stand on that stage and talk about my passion for young girls' inner health and wellbeing, I plunged into self-loathing. This resulted in frustration and anger, and was then mirrored back to me by my children. At the heart of all of it was a fear of being seen, of stepping out to serve an even wider audience. One night, after getting angry with my eldest son earlier in the night, I lay in bed and felt a hatred for myself rise up, its ugliness and darkness strong and powerful. I have never in my life experienced the sense of utter self-loathing I felt in that moment and, for a split-second, a desire to self-harm appeared. Luckily for me, my years of healing and learning had prepared me for this moment and I knew that some deep wound had been triggered and was ready to be released. That knowledge prevented me from actioning those strong and powerful feelings.

The next day I contacted a healer friend for help. It immediately made me feel better and she worked on me to clear and release those feelings and heal that wound. I knew that if I did not face it and work through it that I would sabotage my talk and my chance at breaking through fears that would hold me back in life and in my business. My friend told me that everything I had done in the last eight years and, in fact, over my entire life, had prepared me for this moment. I was ready, more than ready, to take flight.

So it was that on an autumn Sunday, I made my big leap, stepping out onto the main stage under the beautiful dome of the Royal Exhibition Building in Melbourne. I was nervous but loved standing up on stage talking from my heart, telling people what makes my heart sing, sharing my passion and vision with whomever was willing to listen. The same friend said that, for me, it was akin to standing on top of the Eiffel Tower and jumping off. I felt I had made a big breakthrough.

There is now no going back into the shadows. I am no longer at the top of the Eiffel Tower, standing back, hiding, too scared to take a step forward or a step off. After my talk, I felt exhilarated, I felt strong and I felt a deep connection to my passion and my purpose. It truly was time for me to fly.

Of course, the Universe soon let me know that I was not quite ready. Yes, I was ready to fly but I was not ready to soar. Two weeks after that speech, I noticed that I started to resist new opportunities to really step forward and get my message out into the world. Then – wham – there it was, my true belief revealing itself. I was having a conversation with a trainer called Tanya prior to attending her media training workshop, and out from my very own mouth came a belief that said it all: 'If I show who I am I will be cut down'.

As the experiences behind the creation of that belief rose up (and continued to rise up over the next 24 hours), I was shocked at how raw I felt. I thought I had dealt with this issue pretty well previously, and that I had, for the most part, cleared it – enough that it would not hold me back. But, clearly, I had not succeeded. Tanya asked, 'Are you ready to push through it and clear it once and for all?'. I loved that Tanya spoke so honestly. She advised me that if I did not clear it, the success of my business was unlikely to be achieved. You cannot hide away and expect to get your message out there to the world at the same time.

I made a decision right there and then that, yes, as scary as it felt, I was ready to push through it. I knew that there was no going back, but that wounded part of me, the young girl, and the adult, felt the fear of rejection, exclusion, attacks, non-acceptance. Ultimately, the drive towards realising my dreams and living a meaningful, authentic life that's true to who I am won out, as it always has.

The next morning I woke up feeling, in my very core, that no more will I hide and not be all that I am. No more will I silently apologise for being who I am. No more will I keep quiet and not share the passion and the message that burns so strongly within my heart.

When others find they cannot be in my presence because of who I am, no more will I think there is something wrong with me or that I need to be better or do better. I will no longer silently apologise for having the gifts that I was born with.

In my past I have been excluded and attacked, and felt very lonely because I was a good student, because I did really well at many sports, because I was kind, because I got along well with everyone (the popular boys included) and because I was confident.

I have been rejected and betrayed by those closest to me because I chose to start living and speaking my truth, because I chose to listen to my heart's yearning, because I chose to stop living an illusion or living each day by acting on 'I should', and because I chose to let them carry their own fate and their own burdens.

I have chosen to be responsible for myself, my own stuff, my own pain, my own way of being in the world. I have chosen to free myself from all that was keeping me from the truth of who I am. I paid a huge price for making this decision BUT I have never regretted it for a moment. I learned that so much of it was NEVER ABOUT ME. I found myself, I learned to love and accept myself and I freed myself.

I know I have the resources to deal with whatever arises in the future and the fact that I stand tall and strong at 44 years of age confirms that for me. What drives me forward is the possibility of what lies ahead and it always makes the discomfort worth it. I have worked so hard to get myself to this place and there is no compromise anymore.

I am excited about what lies ahead and am working on standing in my feminine – relaxing, allowing, receiving, connecting to my feelings, my body and my sexuality. I am ready to love big and love fearlessly.

Despite some nerves about 'how', I have a quiet confidence and belief in my vision, and a passion that is a fire burning brightly in my belly. I am ready to take flight and soar, even with the knowledge that I may temporarily clip my own wings when another layer arises, asking to be healed. I am ready to be seen and to use the gifts that I have been given to fulfil my dreams, to give meaning to the pain and to hopefully make a difference in someone's life.

For You to Ponder

- Are you at a point in your life when you feel ready to take flight and soar high, to realise your dreams?

- If you have already taken flight, have you paused and acknowledged the courage that it took to step off the edge of the precipice and fly?

- If you have previously taken flight, what happened when you took that step? Can you reflect on anything you learned along the way?

Chapter 20
What Is the Meaning of It All?

'Stop searching the world for treasure, the real treasure is in yourself.'

~ Pablo Valle

Some would say that I analyse and think too much and that may be true on occasions, but I am, by nature, someone who searches for meaning. I have accepted that I look beyond the surface to see what it is I am meant to learn, how am I meant to grow, how I can be better and how I can do better.

When I reflect back over the last 44 years, there are so many major life events that have helped to shape who I am today. Starting with my brother Andrew's death, Ash Wednesday, Dad's multiple sclerosis diagnosis, feeling that my family had shut down and then experiencing the wider world through travel. Then, discovering a deep connection with France, the birth of my children, the breakdown of my marriage, feeling betrayed by my family and breaking off ties, breaking up with my soul mate, creating a new melody for my life, and the conscious healing journey that I have undertaken.

These experiences have all helped me to grow, and to open my heart to myself and others, and they have gifted me with much to be grateful for. The culmination of all of these things has been the realisation of my purpose and the birth of my business.

I offer this summary of the wisdom and learning I have gained through *Finding Freedom... Finding Me*. I hope that this list offers you reassurance and a sense of hope if you are currently experiencing pain and confusion.

I have discovered...

- That we are born with everything we need within us
- That all of us are ultimately wanting the same thing – to be loved and accepted
- That we need to unlearn all that we are taught in order to come back to the truth of who we are
- That choosing love over fear in every situation makes your heart expand – choose fear instead and your heart closes
- That we are all perfectly imperfect and that is perfect
- That love sometimes means letting go and moving on
- That it is in the pain and darkness that we learn the most about ourselves
- That simple things offer great joy
- That one of the cheapest and easiest ways to find healing is to go out and sit in nature and let her fill you up with what you need

What Is the Meaning of It All?

- That we are more than our thoughts and what our logical mind can perceive
- That feeling your pain is better than holding onto it and ignoring it, for pain is energy and, if left unexpressed, it may manifest as illness, excess weight or aggression towards others
- That you cannot be responsible for the choices that another person makes
- That you cannot fix or rescue anyone but can only be there to support and love them
- That everyone has a story behind the mask that we all wear
- That to have someone hear your story is one of the greatest gifts they can give you
- That you can trust your intuition and inner knowing
- That it is okay to be you and it is safe to be you
- That family are not always those who have the same blood running through their veins as you
- That we all do the best we can with what we know at the time
- That you are not alone – love is all around you if you choose to open your eyes and see it
- That there is always something to be grateful for, no matter how dark it may seem

- That carrying your story and past around is like lugging excess baggage up a steep flight of stairs – it is exhausting. When you free yourself from the baggage you gain back energy and your *joie de vivre*.
- That there are always signposts and signals to guide you onto the right path
- That everyone has their own journey to travel in life and each person's fate is their own to carry
- That it is worth opening your heart to love
- That everyone is a fellow traveller in this journey we call life

There have been moments when I have needed to draw upon every ounce of my inner strength and courage to keep myself from drowning. The irony is that all of my experiences have gifted me with that strength and courage.

What I see now is that all of my trauma, pain, challenges, obstacles and heartbreak form the background of the rich tapestry that is my life. Now what I get to do – and the thought of this fills me with a deep sense of anticipation – is to weave the foreground of that tapestry in my own way, with vibrant colour based on my new melody, my new story – one that has taken 44 years to birth.

The Power of Journaling: A Guide to Getting Started

I'd highly recommend using your journal to reflect on the questions throughout the book and in the following 'For You to Delve Deeper…' chapter.

However, if you've ever been a little intimidated by the idea of journaling, I've created a special 'how-to' guide for you that reveals my experience of journaling, and offers suggestions for how journaling can work for you.

When I lived in and travelled around Europe in 1999 and 2000, I kept a journal of the places that I visited, the food that I ate, and my thoughts about what I experienced. I love that I have this journal to refer to and that I can share it with my boys.

I began to journal, sporadically, about my day-to-day life prior to the beginning of my healing journey in 2006. I would miss months at a time, and when I look back now to certain time periods, I wish that I'd recorded my thoughts and feelings more regularly. I took up journal-writing more seriously when I travelled to France in 2012, and by the end of 2013 I had made a vow to make journaling a daily part of my evening, before-bed ritual.

It is the place where I pour my heart and soul onto the pages, writing about how I feel and what I am grateful for each day. In doing so, I have often found the answer to a question that has been tossing around my mind. As I let go and allow the words to flow, the real underlying reason for my feelings will rise up from the page – the divine wisdom spilling forth like nectar. I have found journaling to be a powerful tool in my healing process, and I can feel the difference within me when I slip and don't write in my journal daily – the anxiety builds and I lose the connection to my heart wisdom.

I invite you, and encourage you, to begin journaling. Don't place pressure on yourself to 'get it right'; just begin with one small step. In my opinion, there is no right or wrong way to journal. I am just sharing what has worked for me.

Here are some tips and suggestions to help you get started:

1. Go shopping and choose a journal. I love to choose one with a beautiful cover – I don't mind if it's a plain cover, as long as the colour resonates with me at the time.
2. Set aside time each day (I write at night before I go to sleep) – it can be 10 minutes, it can be half an hour or longer.

3. Find a place in which to sit and write, undisturbed. I generally write in my bed, but I have taken my journal and pen to the beach, out into the garden and to a café – I stay in tune with how I am feeling and go with the flow accordingly.
4. Perhaps record the date – I always write the day, month and year of my entry.
5. Take a few deep breaths to calm and still yourself.
6. If you don't know how to start, simply begin by writing what you did that day – with as much or little description as you like.
7. Alternatively, write down how you are feeling in that moment – for example, I have written just recently, 'Today I feel agitated and I don't really want to be writing in here tonight'.
8. Then let the pen flow – it doesn't matter if your words make no sense when you re-read them. What matters is that you have expressed what is inside of you.
9. Try to write as if no one will ever read it – this should be the case anyway, unless you decide otherwise. These will be your innermost thoughts and feelings, and to get the most out of the process it's best to just relax and write whatever comes to you.
10. You may pose questions to yourself to help you work through current issues. For example, when the belief

arose that I would be cut down if I spoke out and showed myself to the world, I wrote, 'What am I afraid of?' and allowed the answer to come. I wrote that answer down and then wrote, 'If the thing I am afraid of actually occurred, what would really happen?'… the answer then came. Posing questions and waiting for answers allows you to use your journal to go deeper into an issue and to discover the gold.
11. Consider ending your daily entry with, 'Gratitude today for: ……' and list three things for which you are grateful. Even if, on those dark days, you are simply grateful to have a roof over your head and food in the fridge. This practice will help you to see that there are always blessings to be found in your life.

Remember: this is your journal – have fun, leave expectations and judgements about your writing skills out of the experience, and see it as a partner with whom you share your journey.

For You to Delve Deeper...

Throughout this book I included 'For You to Ponder' sections that invited you to reflect on the themes in each chapter.

If you'd like to delve even deeper, in this chapter I pose more questions for you to consider in your own time and in your own way. They are all questions that I have considered and answered as part of my journey. I am no different to you, and I wanted to share questions that have helped me – if you choose, you can develop your own curiosity about who you really are and begin a journey towards finding your own freedom.

Feel free to start (or continue) your journaling journey by pondering the following questions – below each question I offer my own perspectives, in the hope that my view inspires you or helps you in some way.

Do you put everyone else before you, all or most of the time?
As women it seems that we feel guilty if we put ourselves first or before others. Why do we feel selfish? I have learned that if we put ourselves first and look after our needs without feeling guilty, we are bestowing a huge gift on those around us. I have noticed that when I do not take care of myself, when I neglect

to exercise or take time to do things that I really want to do, I become stressed. As the stress builds, my children feed off it. However, when I do all of those things and more, I feel great and the family runs more smoothly. Everyone is happy. My role model for this is Robin McGraw (wife of TV's Dr Phil), who is a huge advocate of women looking after themselves – and nobody could ever accuse her of being a bad mother or wife!

Do you teach others that you matter?

I have learned, the hard way, that it is up to me to show my boys and others that I matter and deserve to be considered. Earlier this year I was feeling very stressed and did not feel that I was being a good mother. My body was crying out for a run, and by the end of a very busy week, I instinctively knew that I needed the exercise to reduce the stress that I was feeling.

To ensure that I met my need for exercise, I planned on fitting in a run before a 9.30am appointment on the Friday. That morning, I tried to get the boys ready for school and out on time; however, they played up and laughed at me when I asked them to get ready, despite my asking nicely that they hurry up. They were in no mood for listening, and in that moment I felt quite disrespected, and my anger was building. However, as I later pounded the pavement, I had an 'aha' moment – I recognised that unless I voiced my needs to my boys, how would they know that a run was so important to me in terms of my wellbeing?

I realised that I needed to tell them that my inner health and wellbeing was imperative – that, for me to be a good mother and do what I needed to do, I needed to exercise. As such, I needed them to play their part in helping me to achieve that. It was ultimately up to me to teach the boys that I mattered as much as they did.

Do you celebrate your achievements and milestones? What milestones have you achieved that you could celebrate now?
It is important to honour what you have achieved and the milestones that you reach in life. You don't need to hold a party or ritual, but you could set aside some time to get a massage; walk on your favourite beach; take a drive to the country; buy yourself a nice aromatic candle; buy yourself some flowers; take the day off and go to the movies; or really indulge and lie in bed all day, reading a book. Give back to yourself by doing something you love to do – show appreciation for your efforts and all that you have gone through.

Is sensuality a part of your life?
I do not necessarily mean sensuality in a sexual way. Do you use all of your senses, as a woman? I love inhaling the aroma of fresh flowers, scented candles and essential oils. I love using lamps and tea-light candles in various candleholders to provide a soft and calming ambience at night-time. I love lying in a bubble

bath, a candle the only light, the warm water caressing my skin, the bubbles providing a sense of luxury, and the subtle scent of white jasmine from the bath oil emanating up to my nose. I love the feeling of silk against my skin, and how it makes me feel sexy and feminine when I wear my beautiful crimson slip at night. There are so many ways to awaken your senses to help connect you to the feminine part of yourself.

I encourage you to awaken your sensuality – to tap into the pleasure and power of your feminine essence – by trying some or all of the following:

- Buy yourself a bunch of fresh, scented flowers.
- Burn a scented candle while relaxing in a warm bath.
- Take off your shoes and walk in bare feet upon the grass or sand at the beach, taking time to become aware of how it feels on your skin.
- Close your eyes the next time you eat a strawberry, or your favourite fruit, chocolate or treat – take your time eating it, let your other senses take over, and see what you notice.
- Put on your favourite music, close your eyes and dance – be mindful of how it feels in your body to move.
- Sit in your garden, a park or at the beach and close your eyes. What do you hear?
- The next time you have a coffee or a cup of tea, slow down when you make it – take in the sound of the water

For You to Delve Deeper...

as it flows into the cup, leave the coffee in your mouth long enough to appreciate the depth of flavour, savour each mouthful...
- Go outside after it has rained. What do you smell? What does the world around you look like?
- If you don't normally wear a dress or skirt, stretch yourself and put one on. How does it make you feel, as a woman? (I used to struggle with wearing dresses, but as my feminine essence has emerged more and more, I have fallen in love with them.)
- Give yourself a massage (feet, hands, legs, arms, shoulders) – take your time and perform it with reverence and love for yourself and your body.
- The next time you apply body lotion or cream after a bath or shower, slow down. Massage it in, caress your body, feel the pleasure in giving to yourself.
- Eat a healthier diet and exercise – notice how you feel when you do – there should be an increased energy and vitality.

Do you own some lovely lingerie, bought just because it makes you feel good?
I decided a couple of years ago to splurge and purchase some beautiful lingerie made from French lace and silk, just for me – to help make me feel good about myself as a woman. I didn't

want to wait until a man came into my life and then buy it only to give pleasure to him. I wanted to experience that pleasure for myself, simply because I deserved it. I make sure that I wear it on normal days and not just save it for when I go out or for a special occasion.

Is there any space for a man to be the man in your life?
I am a strong and independent woman who can do anything I put my mind to. However, one day my therapist said to me, 'If you are busy doing everything, what is there left for a man to do? He will have nothing to offer you or the relationship'. Wow! That really resonated with me, so I made a decision, in that moment, that I did not need to prove myself any longer. I knew what I was capable of but I would start practising asking a man for help when I needed it – and I loved it! It felt good to let go of that need to show that I was capable.

When you next feel overwhelmed and out of balance, are you willing to sit quietly and ask yourself what you need in that moment?
I have learned to use these moments to try to tune in to why I am feeling overwhelmed and what it is that I really need. It may be that I need to talk through the issue with someone and have them reflect back to me what I am feeling. It may be that I need to take some time out and do something for myself that gives

For You to Delve Deeper...

me joy – for me, this often means visiting my favourite café and bookshop. It may be that I need to get out and move, go for a walk and shift my energy. It may be that I have said yes too many times and overloaded myself.

Circle of Gratitude: Creating Your Own Ceremony

To honour the women who have made a positive impact on your life, I encourage you to hold your own Circle of Gratitude. I encourage you to do it now, before it may be too late to acknowledge certain people.

I didn't wait until I was 'healed' or 'ready' to gather women to share my gratitude with them. I also didn't have great relationships with everyone I invited but that did not mean that they hadn't made a deep impact on me at some point – this is a chance to lay down the ego and any issues you may have and let your heart lead the way.

Preparing for Your Circle of Gratitude Ceremony

1. Sit down and think about the women in your life and who has made a deep impact on you.
2. Make a list of potential guests – keeping it to fewer than 10 women (for example, I had seven women present

and included my therapist, my sister-in-law who had looked after my boys during the early days of my family betrayal, and my beloved aunt). A small number of guests means that the ceremony will be intimate, and it allows you time to share what each guest means to you without the day/evening going on for too long.
3. Set the date and prepare the invitations – choose beautiful paper and envelopes.
4. Make sure the house will be clear of partners and children!

Ideas to Make It Special

1. As this is also a celebration of you, consider how you can set up the physical space for the ceremony so that you feel at peace in it and it reflects you.
2. I'd highly recommend buying your favourite flowers and having a special candle (or candles) burning.
3. Consider providing each woman with a small token of your gratitude. Perhaps a handwritten card or note with the words you spoke out loud written on it, or perhaps a photo of the two of you together. Let it be something that holds meaning for you.
4. Have your favourite foods to share.
5. Speak from your heart and let the ceremony be a reflection of you, your love and gratitude.

Circle of Gratitude: Creating Your Own Ceremony

I suggest that your Circle of Gratitude only include women (rather than men), as a way for all of you to connect to the feminine essence – which embodies qualities such as nurturing, wisdom and sharing – and to ensure that others' views on males do not encroach upon the sacredness of the ceremony you have created. There is, however, no reason why you could not have a Circle of Gratitude for the important men in your life if you felt that this was right for you.

My Heartfelt Thanks

'Gratitude is the fairest blossom which springs from the soul.'

~ Henry Ward Beecher

Firstly, I feel so proud and honoured to be the mother of the two most amazing and precious souls in my life – James and Liam. You are both my constant inspiration and motivation to dig deeper, to fight the fear, to break down the walls, to dissolve the patterns of generations. I am so grateful that you chose to walk with me on this journey, that you so graciously support me as I follow my soul's calling to France even though you both miss me terribly. I am grateful that you show me constantly by your behaviour and with your voice that which I still need to work on. I am truly blessed and I cannot wait to share the rewards of all of this hard work with you, for you to see that life is not all about pain and challenges.

My beautiful editor, book consultant/publisher and partner in the birthing of this book, Joanne Newell. I believe that God guided you to me in another moment of grace. In you he gave me someone whose heart and soul connected with mine, whom I knew was going to treat my story and my vision with as much reverence as if it were your own. You have encouraged me and guided me along a path that was unfamiliar and daunting and you did it with much love and support. I believe that I held off on the writing of my book until you came along, and I know that without you I could not have delivered what I have.

To Amy De Wolfe for her luscious book cover design. You captured the essence perfectly. Thank you also for all of your work in the illustration, layout and marketing materials for the book.

Enormous gratitude to my healing team, who have helped me find freedom and find myself. I have the utmost respect for all of their own journeys and the moments at which they went above and beyond to help me, often at short notice – Susanne, Grant, Arte Ma, Sonya, Anna, Daniel, The Awakening Group, Belinda and Susan.

Something that has touched my heart deeply is the connection I have made with some beautiful women. Some I call my sisters.

These women are my 'soul family'. They have held me up in moments when the weight of darkness has almost crushed me. They have helped me to learn to laugh again. They have supported me, encouraged me and cried with me. Their belief in me has never wavered and I am grateful that they held onto that belief when I could not see anything of value in myself and did not believe that I had anything to offer.

They have shown me that it is safe to trust women again,

My Heartfelt Thanks

that there is power and sacredness in healthy and authentic female friendships, that I can speak my truth and still be considered a friend. They have shown me how important it is as women to support, encourage and nurture each other. I feel incredibly emotional when I think about what these women mean to me. They have brought great healing and love into my life.

So, to my precious 'soul sisters', I say thank you – Kimberley, Josephine, Tanya and Susan. Your presence has been one of the greatest gifts I have ever received.

To my beautiful girlfriends, who are also part of my soul family and who have journeyed with me and supported me, thank you – Jo C, Kristin, Susanne, Karen, Lisa V, Sonya, Nicole and Hulya. To anyone I have forgotten, my deepest apologies.

To the group of amazing women and facilitators, particularly Brenda Sutherland, who journeyed with me in 2014 on the Certificate of Holistic Counselling course. My heart is filled with a profound gratitude for the space you held that enabled me to venture into the depths of my pain. A space that was safe and loving and contained a vibration of healing energy. You are all amazing and an integral part of my story, always.

Daniel Sowelu from Sacred Law Firm for holding experiential astrology courses that took me deeper into the archetypes that were distorted and in the way, so that I could release ancient rage, sexual trauma, grief, fear and more. To those fellow participants who have stepped into the ring with me on more than one occasion – Bec, Chris, Martina, Sabrina, Zac, Stefan – and to the others who have held the space, I am so very grateful. I admire your courage in taking the same journey.

To the angels who were sent my way to help remove my remaining limiting beliefs, who encouraged me, who helped me relaunch my business under my own name, who believed in me and drove me forward to achieve the vision for this book – Robyn W, Johannah, Stacey, Tanya C-T and Rose – thank you for being a part of a project that I hope will make a difference in someone's life.

To my ex-husband and father to my boys. Thank you for sharing many of my treasured memories that were created as we lived and travelled overseas. Thank you for being a continued support and for joining me in putting the wellbeing and needs of our boys before our own issues. Thank you for believing in me and supporting me so that I could achieve my dream of publishing this book. My hope has always been that you would find happiness and love once more. While we are no longer a daily part of each other's lives, I could not imagine you not being a part of mine at all.

To my ex-husband's family – thank you for never taking sides, for always being there for the boys and me. I have never taken for granted how fortunate I am.

In memory of my Auntie Judy, who, sadly, is not here to witness the realisation of my dreams. Thank you for always believing in me, for being there for me and for encouraging me to follow my heart. You set me on my path of healing – I just wish you were here to share my journey with me – to see that I made it through the darkness. However, I know that you can see me and are still there for me. Much love.

To the spiritual guideposts I received along the way: whether they were books recommended to me, books that jumped off the shelf into my hand, television shows that I was guided to watch, workshops that I attended or quotes that appeared just when I needed them. For all those who created these guideposts, so that they may impact the lives of others, thank you.

Heartfelt thanks go to my family: despite the distance, I love each and every one of you. I thank you for all of the moments that pushed me, challenged me, pained me. Ultimately, I consider them to be acts of love for it all brought me to this place where, today, I am fulfilling my purpose in life. Without all of that I would not be able to do what I do and I would not have come home to myself. I hope that on a soul level you feel this love and know that my heart beats with compassion and gratitude daily.

And finally to my mother. I know that you loved us all, showing this by cooking for us, making our clothes, driving us to our sporting activities, and more. That you loved us I will never deny, and I know, because you said it many times, that you would have done anything to protect us from physical harm. I am grateful for all that you taught me in the kitchen – how to 'cream butter and sugar', how to make jam and chutney, Christmas pudding and more. I observed the pain you were in and the effect it had on those around you. I have chosen to respond to my pain in a different way, for me and for my children. I sincerely hope that you find inner peace – your fate is yours to carry and I leave it with you now. I will always respect that it is your decision as to how you respond to, and deal with, your pain. I will always hold love for you in my heart.

My Healing Team

I could not have healed my pain without the help of many others. These are the amazing people who shared their healing abilities with me:

Susanne Calman
Feminine Spirit
www.femininespirit.com.au

Dr Grant Lambert
Advanced Alchemy
www.qualityessences.com

Anna Fry
Kinesiologist/Reiki Master/Teacher
www.annafry.org

Susan Morrow
www.susanmorrow.com.au

Arte'ma
Sacred Nature
www.sacrednature.com.au

Sonya Edmonds
Mother Nurture
www.mothernurture.net.au

Belinda Aquilina
Belaqua's Massage Therapy
www.belaquasmassagetherapy.com.au

The Awakening Group
www.awakening.com.au

Daniel Sowelu
Sacred Law Firm
www.sacredlawfirm.com.au

Feed Your Mind & Soul

Following is a selection of some of the many books that I have read and websites that I have consulted since my healing journey began. I recommend them should you wish to expand your knowledge of any of the topics listed.

Spirituality & Esoteric Knowledge

- *The Power of Now* by Eckhart Tolle
- *A New Earth* by Eckhart Tolle
- *A Return to Love* by Marianne Williamson
- *The Power of Intention* by Dr Wayne Dyer
- *Living in the Heart* by Drunvalo Melchizedek
- *Wheels of Life* by Anodea Judith
- *The Sevenfold Journey* by Anodea Judith & Selene Vega
- *Eastern Body, Western Mind* by Anodea Judith
- *The Seven Spiritual Laws of Success for Parents* by Deepak Chopra
- *Care of the Soul* by Thomas Moore
- *The Seat of the Soul* by Gary Zukav

Healing/General

- *Eat, Pray, Love* by Elizabeth Gilbert
- *Women's Bodies, Women's Wisdom* by Dr Christiane Northrup
- *The Wisdom of Menopause* by Dr Christiane Northrup
- *What I know for Sure* by Oprah Winfrey
- *Daring Greatly* by Brené Brown
- *Loving What Is* by Byron Katie
- *Fear* by Thich Nhat Hanh
- *The Road Less Travelled* by M Scott Peck
- *You Can Heal Your Life* by Louise Hay
- *The Secret Language of Your Body* by Inna Segal

The Black Madonna

- *The Cult of the Black Virgin* by Ean Begg

The Cathars

- *The Cathars & Reincarnation* by Arthur Guirdham
- *The Cathars* by (Société) MSM

Mary Magdalene/Divine Feminine

- *The Gospel of Mary Magdalene* by Jean-Yves Leloup
- *Mary Magdalene Beckons – Join the River of Love* by Mercedes Kirkel

- *Sublime Union* by Mercedes Kirkel
- *The Expected One, The Book of Love and The Poet Prince – a trilogy* by Kathleen McGowan
- *14 Steps to Awaken the Sacred Feminine* by Joan Norton & Margaret Starbird
- *Mary Magdalene and the Divine Feminine – Jesus' Lost Teachings on Women* by Elizabeth Clare Prophet

Family Constellations

- Hellinger Sciencia
  www.hellinger.com

- Family Constellations
  www.familyconstellations.com.au

- The Hellinger Institute of Northern California
  www.hellingerpa.com

About the Author

Jody Kalpenos is a feminine connection mentor who helps women to hear the calling of their hearts, and to re-discover their dreams, desires, sensuality and *joie de vivre*.

Jody feels blessed to live in Melbourne, Australia, with her two young sons. She connects with her own feminine essence by reading inspiring books, heading out into fresh country air, inhaling the scent of garden-picked roses, savouring sumptuous food, honouring her intuition, engaging in meaningful conversations, boogying to ABBA and winging her way across blue waters to France.

She is an inspiring, captivating speaker and hosts small boutique tours to France, as well as offering events and meditations to help women re-connect with their feminine essence. You can discover more about Jody and her heart-filled services at www.jodykalpenos.com.

> *'Journey with me as we connect with the land, people, energy, spirit and magic of Paris and Provence in an authentic and feminine way.'*
>
> ~ Jody Kalpenos

If you've resonated with my story and you, too, adore the energy of France, then I invite you to join me on a small boutique tour of Paris and Provence.

On this 11-day tour, we begin in Paris… the City of Love and Light… where we experience French elegance, beauty and a few things girly. We then take the train to the south of France… and settle into our own private villa just five minutes from St Remy de Provence.

Here we awaken our senses, nurturing our mind, body and soul – touring, relaxing, savouring beautiful meals cooked by our private chef, tastings of the local wines, markets, a picnic, shopping, history and more… This leisurely tour allows you to truly connect with the feminine within you. There will be plenty of time for you to slow down, relax… and breathe!

**To discover more about this special tour –
and other tours to France
that I have curated for you – please visit:**

www.jodykalpenos.com

Review Request

Dear Reader

Did you resonate with this book or feel inspired to begin your own journey to freedom? If so, I'd be very grateful if you'd post an honest review so that we begin to build a community of women who share and understand each other's stories. Your review may just be the words that inspire change in another woman's life and be the very thing that sets her on her own journey to freedom.

To leave a review, simply go to the review section on the Amazon page for *Finding Freedom... Finding Me*. Click on the big button that says 'Write a customer review' and you're good to go!

May we all help inspire greatness in each other.

Yours in love and light

Jody x